CLASSICS
OF
ANCIENT
CHINA

For Mark HAUSER,

Thank You! for

turning me on to ~~Specific/Verbal~~ the nameless TAO. just like the water ~~academic~~ ~~telling~~ ~~TAO~~ the fish about waves. and the Chuang Tzu. and chess and canoes and long talks. and home made mabo Tofu w/ Buns and paper Dragons... —Brian

YUAN DAO:
TRACING *DAO*
TO ITS SOURCE

Translated by

D. C. Lau

and

Roger T. Ames

With an introduction by

Roger T. Ames

BALLANTINE BOOKS
THE BALLANTINE PUBLISHING GROUP
NEW YORK

A Ballantine Book
The Ballantine Publishing Group

http://www.randomhouse.com

Library of Congress Cataloging-in-Publication Data
Huai-nan tzu. 1. Yüan tao. English.
        Tracing Dao to its source / translated by D. C. Lau and Roger T. Ames : with an introduction by Roger T. Ames. — 1st ed.
        p.   cm. — (Classics of ancient China)
        Includes bibliographical references (p. 151).
        ISBN 0–345–42568–5 (alk. paper)
        1. Lau, D. C. (Din Cheuk) II. Ames, Roger T., 1947–
III. Title. IV. Series.
BL1900.H822E5   1998
181'.114—dc21

                                                97–52299
                                                CIP

Cover design by Carlos Beltrán

Manufactured in the United States of America

First Edition: August 1998

10   9   8   7   6   5   4   3   2   1

CONTENTS

We would like to acknowledge our indebtedness to Daniel Cole and Ho Che Wah 何志華, who from different continents have lent different yet always exceptional technical skills to the realization of our project. Both of our editors, Robert G. Henricks and Owen Lock, brought a critical gaze to bear upon the interpretation of *Tracing* Dao *to Its Source*, occasioning some substantial changes. We think it is a better book for their efforts, but remain responsible ourselves for its ultimate message.

D. C. Lau (Hong Kong)
Roger T. Ames (Hawai'i)

PART ONE:

INTRODUCTION

THE *HUAINANZI* AND THE COURT OF EMPEROR WU

Tracing Dao *to Its Source* (*yuandao* 原道) is the opening treatise of the *Huainanzi* 淮南子. The *Huainanzi* is an early-Han-dynasty (late-second-century BCE) compendium of knowledge which covers every subject from astronomy and calendrics to government and the art of warfare. The early part of the Han dynasty was a formative period in what we might call "Han thinking"—a syncretic way of thinking and living that came, and continues, to be characteristically "Chinese." And *Tracing* Dao *to Its Source* is among the earliest and most seminal of the documents that illustrate how Han thinkers came to see their world.

With some confidence, the *Huainanzi* can be dated to about 139 BCE and the central court of Emperor Wu (r. 141–87 BCE) of the Han dynasty 漢武帝. This compendium was probably presented to Emperor Wu by his vassal and paternal uncle, Liu An 劉安, the king of Huainan, as a gift to celebrate Emperor Wu's succession to the dragon throne of the recently unified Chinese empire. But there was a purpose to this gift: to teach the young emperor how to understand the world around him. Liu An was celebrated as a man of letters whose stature was established by gathering at his own court ranking philosophes of his age to reflect upon all matters great and small as they shaped the world of his time. Out of these reflections a library of texts was produced that came to dominate his court and to animate the intellectual life of the dynasty.

The historical context is important to our understanding of the *Huainanzi*.[1] With the collapse of the short-lived Qin dynasty in the last decade of the third century BCE, the empire sank into a protracted period of civil war. As Liu Bang 劉邦, the founding father of the Han dynasty, rose to emperor against the competing confederation of Xiang Yu, he expediently allowed the self-proclaimed kings who had supported him in his campaign to retain control over their lands. Thus, his "empire" in 202 BCE was a tenuous lamination of fourteen commanderies in the west over which he exercised direct control, and ten kingdoms to the east under the command of vassal kings. At the same time, the entire empire was under constant threat from incursions of Xiongnu tribes on the borderlands. Over the century that followed, it became a central task of the Han court to disenfranchise these vassal kings and consolidate its own power at their expense.

The first stage was for the emperor to replace the vassal kings with family members loyal to his blood line. This happened quickly, but was by no means effective. By 196 BCE, nine of the ten kingdoms had been placed under the control of an imperial relative. However, the passage of time together with contention among family members for the imperial throne served to dilute the loyalty expected by the central court, and to fuel the forces of separatism and disintegration. Further measures were necessary to reduce the threat of rebellion.

Over a period of decades, a conscious strategy was implemented to reduce the size and strength of these kingdoms, and to take advantage of any and all reasons available to the emperor to first divide them up into smaller kingdoms, and then ultimately to redefine them into imperial commanderies. In fact, in 154 BCE, some ten years after Liu An came to power in Huainan, seven of his fellow kings joined in a revolt against the imperial court, but succeeded only in providing it with a pretext for accelerating its process of centralization.

It was under these circumstances that Liu An ruled the kingdom of Huainan, already much diminished from the original polity that had flourished as a major power in the early days of the Han empire. It was with the specter of imminent annexation hanging over his court that he went about the business of the day.

Thus, there is a great personal tragedy that is remembered in this gift to Emperor Wu. When Emperor Wu was first embarking on his reign of "all under the heavens," Liu An was a favorite uncle of the young emperor, and was widely respected as a patron of learning by the imperial family and the existing academy. The central message of *Tracing Dao to Its Source*, and the *Huainanzi* broadly, is philosophical. It advocates inclusivity—an appreciation of the contribution that each and every thing can make to the well-being of the whole when orchestrated by able leadership into a productive harmony. Practically speaking, the text is a political statement of this same pluralistic idea. While *Huainanzi* taken as a whole is syncretic, *Tracing Dao to Its Source* is a cloaked but compelling Daoistic argument against political centralism, expansionism, and the zero-sum consolidation of power that was driving the imperial court during this first century of the Han dynasty.

Intellectually, the vassal court of Liu An can, in retrospect, be seen as a feudal bastion of pluralistic shamanism and "Daoistic" culture holding out against the gradual ascendancy of a state Confucianism which was to become the central ideology under the growing influence of scholar-statesmen such as Jia Yi (200–169 BCE), Chao Cuo (d. 154 BCE), and Dong Zhongshu (179–104 BCE). While Jia Yi and particularly Chao Cuo can hardly be described as undiluted advocates of Confucian values, their main message to the throne—curtail the power of the kings—did serve the interests of political centralism. In fact, it was this message that, in the swim of court politics, cost both of them their lives. It was thus left to Dong Zhongshu to make the argument for the Confucian alternative to more stringent legalistic policies.

Less than two decades after taking the throne in 141 BCE, the now supremely powerful Emperor Wu, whose posthumous title of "martial emperor (*wudi* 武帝)" he so richly deserved, was inextricably caught up in the drive toward centralized empire. In 122 BCE, accusing Liu An of lèse-majesté, he demanded that his uncle appear before him to answer the charge of inciting rebellion. It is possible that Liu An in desperation tried to launch a preemptive strike against the inevitable eclipse of his kingdom, or even more likely that such accusations were fabricated in order to lay claim to one of the final political pieces that might resist the emperor's authority. In any case, Liu An was forced into his final move. Liu An's suicide (or execution) allowed Emperor Wu to arrest his family members and loyal retainers at the Shouchun 壽春 capital of Huainan, and to rid this world of any would-be successors. To this end, the central court conducted speedy hearings on the charge of treason followed predictably by mass executions, and in the process, laid its own claim to the remaining lands of Huainan. Liu An's name was stricken from the family register of the imperial house, thus ostensibly erasing him from the official lineage.

This tragic end of the literatus Liu An and the treason that came to be associated with his name might be the clue necessary to explain the hotly debated yet still mysterious relationship between the *Huainanzi* and a second Han dynasty text clearly based upon it, the *Wenzi*. The contemporary scholar Ho Che Wah 何志華 has proffered a plausible scenario. The "execution" of the king of Huainan as a traitor to the throne in 122 BCE likely had a rather numbing effect on the circulation of a text that bore his name, at least throughout the long reign of Emperor Wu (d. 87 BCE). For this reason, some of its contents were appropriated and edited into a second volume and circulated under the name of *Wenzi*.[2] In a literary culture in which it was common for one text to borrow freely and liberally from another, the kinship between the suspended *Huainanzi* and its close cousin, the *Wenzi*, would not necessarily draw official condemnation, especially given the conflicted relationship Emperor Wu had with his literary uncle.

As philosophical literature, *Tracing* Dao *to Its Source* can be judged
against the standard set by the early Daoist classics, the *Daodejing* 道德
經 and the *Zhuangzi* 莊子 . In philosophical content and in style, it is
to be most immediately identified as a practical extension of these earlier Daoist ("Lao-Zhuang") texts, frequently alluding to them directly,
and providing further reflection on their central theme: How are we to
understand the dynamic world that gives us context, and how are we to
function effectively within our ever changing social, political, cultural,
and natural environments? Or perhaps more to the point, how does
the world hang together, and how are we to make the most of it? In our
translation of *Tracing* Dao *to Its Source,* we have noted direct allusions
to the *Daodejing* and the *Zhuangzi* to illustrate the intimate relationship to these Daoist texts.

In the *Huainanzi,* Daoism serves as a primary ore, being alloyed
with the concerns and perspectives of competing schools to produce a
more malleable and practical amalgam. The coherence of the
Huainanzi, however, is one true to the spirit of Lao-Zhuang in that
conflicting and divided opinions are happily juxtaposed as necessary to
provide for the fullest summary of China's literary culture. It is rich-
ness and intensity, rather than some rationalized order, that are the
signature of *Huainanzi*'s version of syncretic Daoism.

The *Summary* postface 要略 at the end of the *Huainanzi,* perhaps
written by its compiler, Liu An himself, describes the contents of *Tracing* Dao *to Its Source* in the following terms:

> *Tracing* Dao *to Its Source* takes the measure of the world in all di-
> rections, explores the inchoate origins of the myriad things, traces
> out the lines of its grand continuities, and probes the mysteries of
> what is hidden and obscure, thereby taking one soaring beyond
> the carriage crossbar into the realm of nothingness. By investing
> in what is small it embraces what is great, and by guarding what is
> concise it brings proper order to what is expansive. It enables a

person to understand the consequences of either taking the lead or following behind, and what is advantageous or at risk in either taking action or remaining still. To master its message is to have access to a grand view of things on a truly panoramic scale. If one wants to capture its message in a phrase, it is to defer to what is natural and to preserve one's genuineness. If one wants to illumine its message with a second phrase, it is to take external things lightly and prize one's own person. If one wants a third phrase that gets to its core, it is to externalize things and to return to one's nature as it really is. Grasping its central message, one harmonizes one's internal organs and nourishes one's flesh and skin. If one accepts and complies with its standards and precepts, and lives by them to the end of one's days, it provides a way to respond to and deal with the world around one, and to observe and match changes as they arise. As easy as turning a ball in the palm of one's hand, it enables one to find personal happiness.

This passage restates the central concern of *Tracing* Dao *to Its Source* in the language of Daoism itself: What is the most appropriate and efficacious correlation between the particular detail (*de* 德) and the vastness of the cosmos (*dao* 道), between the excellence of this particular person in this specific situation and the sum of all orders, between one's uniquely focused personal narrative and the dynamics of one's field of experience? It is from this same typically Daoist concern for the productive relationship between particular focus and its extended field that the *Daodejing* takes its title: "the classic of *dao* and *de*."

Implicit in this summary of *Tracing* Dao *to Its Source*, there is an immediate philosophical association between Lao–Zhuang Daoism and the *Huainanzi*, with this latter text borrowing large parts of the earlier works. *Tracing* Dao *to Its Source* frequently cites specific terms from the *Daodejing* and the *Zhuangzi*, providing extended elaborations on the key philosophical vocabulary, for example, *tian* 天 ("Heaven"), *ren* 人 ("man"), *wuwei* 無爲 ("doing nothing"), *wubuwei* 無不爲 ("leaving nothing undone"), *zhiruo* 志弱 ("weak of purpose"), *houzhe* 後者 ("coming behind"), *wuxing* 無形 ("the formless"), *yi* 一 ("the one"), *zide* 自得 ("finding it in oneself"), *you tianxia* 有天下 ("possessing the empire").

The second treatise in the *Huainanzi*, *The Beginning Reality* (*chuzhen* 俶眞), draws heavily upon the *Zhuangzi* with fully a third of its content being borrowed from this single source.[3] In fact, and seldom advertised, the expression "Lao–Zhuang" itself occurs for the first time in the postface to the *Huainanzi*:

> The *Responses to* Dao treatise selects out and gathers together the vestiges of past affairs, and traces out and contemplates what remains of bygone times. It investigates the cycles of calamity and good fortune, of benefit and injury. Experimenting with the arts of Laozi and Zhuangzi ("Lao–Zhuang"), it enables one to accommodate the vicissitudes of life.

"HAN THINKING" AND RADIAL ORDER

Just as the Han court's consolidation of empire was to shape the geographical and political order of the enduring "Han" Chinese for the following two millennia, so its consolidation of a literary tradition was to lay the foundation for the development of Chinese letters for centuries to come. The contribution of the Han dynasty in setting the formal structures of intellectual growth is enormous: the proliferation of official institutions such as imperial libraries and court bureaucracies, the first attempts to compile comprehensive histories, the editing and designation of a literary canon and the beginnings of the commentarial tradition in "the study of the classics" *jingxue* 經學 , the establishment of the long-lived examination system that provided China with its government officials until its final abolition in 1905, the ascendancy of Confucianism as a state ideology which would shape the content of the examination curriculum throughout the life of the empire, and so on.

Neither the Han dynasty texts, nor the early Han world more broadly, evidences the analytical, dialectical, or discursive order with which the Western scholar is most familiar. In fact, understanding

9

Han China requires that, with imagination, we devise a very different strategy for excavating and appreciating the architecture of *Tracing Dao to Its Source*, itself a fair representative of both the *Huainanzi* and Han thinking more broadly. To begin with, the choice of the word "excavating" is probably ill-advised here because it assumes that readers must embark on a process of discovery rather than on a collaborative effort to interpret the text for their own place and time. We will indeed need alternatives to the analytically driven theoretical and conceptual devices that have been privileged in the more systematic Western tradition, where the assumption has been that appearances must be penetrated and set aside as dross in order to comprehend the reality that stands behind them.

The "syncretism" which we generally associate with the Han literary world, and with the *Huainanzi* in particular, is not random or eclectic. The underlying structure of most of the syncretic texts and their commentarial appendices tends to be an illustration of what we will call an emanating and centripetal "radial" order. This radial sensibility is pervasive, defining everything from the process of personal realization to political order. A particular person pursues realization as the center of a circle (*lun* 輪) of familial relationships (*lun* 倫) that are deepened through effective communication (*lun* 論). The fabric of communities (*li* 里), patterned (*li* 理) by a syntax of social relations, emerges out of these overlapping patriarchially organized family circles which are themselves nourished intellectually by local and contemporaneous commentaries contending for proximity to a persistent canonical core (*jing* 經). Scholars in writing annotations and commentaries (*zhu* 注 and *zhu* 註) on these principal texts appeal to the *leishu* 類書 classificatory works which organize the world in circles of graduated value around the life at court. At the same time, court members of the bureaucracy vie for proximity to an imperial center of power. Connecting this court politically with the outside world, the tributary system draws "gifts" from the periphery to "contribute" materially and culturally to an ever changing definition of the "Han."

The *Huainanzi,* as a compendium of knowledge, can serve as a fair example of this Han radial order. The text begins from its "hub" with repeated reflections on tracing *dao* back to its source, a theme from which this opening treatise takes its name. The postface to the *Huai-nanzi* describes the communication of a practical understanding of *dao* as the main objective of those who participated in its compilation:

> Thus, in these twenty treatises, the patterns (*li* 理) of the heavens and the earth are thoroughly explored; the affairs of the human world are broached; the ways of emperors and kings are given full account. This discussion touches upon the huge and the small, upon the most delicate and the much less so. The import of each treatise is different, and each has its own way of expressing its message. Now if the discussion were of *dao* alone, even though *dao* pervades everything and everywhere, it would be the sage alone who could grasp its root and understand its implications. . . . Since discussions of *dao* are so profound, much has to be said about it in order to unfold its real meaning. Because the myriad things are so prolific, observations about them must range broadly in order to disclose their full significance.

Beyond the radial structure of the *Huainanzi* text as a whole, turning as it does on the pivot of *dao,* it is important to give proper notice to the internal impulse that carries the reader from one image to the next. Rhyme patterns, parallel passages, sustained line length, repeated expressions, linking metaphors, expanding hyperbole, the skillful use of tropes—all such literary devices contribute to the rhythmic unfolding of the text.

Often the author of a treatise in the *Huainanzi* will construct an image around a particular character or expression. Either this expression is returned to for further (not necessarily consistent) elaboration, or alternatively, some loosely related image which is suggested in the elaboration itself is pursued. The style of a particular passage will evoke associations with other literature available in the repository of the tradition. Frequently material is carried over from earlier works, or from the memory of earlier works, to be retailored and made meaning-ful for the new context. Echoes abound from the disparate schools of the pre-Qin period, often reshaped to express meanings rather distant from their original import, but deemed relevant to life in the early Han. As such, the pattern of the text is a pastiche—a concatenation of diverse images and allusions, all made important by the reflections of the author on how the world ought to hang together.[4] For the reader, the process of mapping out the geography of the text, separating rhymed passages from parallel text, prose exposition from anecdote, is a necessary first step in the project of coming to understand it.

It is this radial and mosaic structure of the *Huainanzi* that has en-couraged students of Chinese culture to deal with sometimes single and sometimes multiple treatises within the text as "separate" entities. From both a philosophical and a stylistic perspective, the individual treatises reflect fully the diversity one would expect in a text that is the product of many hands. Although there are continuities such as recur-rent themes and an overlapping philosophical vocabularly that belongs to a specific place and time, few scholars would be comfortable with the expression "the philosophy of the *Huainanzi*." There remains some disagreement among interpreters of this text as to whether or not the term "Huang-Lao 黃老" does anything to shed light on the contents of the *Huainanzi* as a whole. The translators of this treatise remain among those who would reserve judgment on its application until we have a clearer idea of what this characterization would entail. At this point in time, "Huang-Lao" has become a receptacle for any early Han dynasty text that has a Daoist tincture, and given the syncretism that marks this period, there is little that is excluded by it.[5]

Much if not most of the scholarship on the *Huainanzi* accom-plished so far within the Western academy, acknowledging the diver-sity of the text, has sought to treat the treatises individually, or at least in related groupings. The story of this research effort is recounted in detail by Charles Le Blanc in the "The Field of *Huai-nan Tzu* Studies" in his *Huai-nan Tzu: Philosophical Synthesis in Early Han Thought* (1985), himself providing a thorough study of the key notion of "resonance (*ganying* 感應)" together with a translation of the *Huainanzi* treatise that most directly expresses it, *Peering into the Obscure* (*lanming* 覽冥).

Two important additions to this project in more recent years have been Harold D. Roth's rigorous study of the transmission of this composite work, *The Textual History of the Huai-nan Tzu* (1992), that has become a model of textual criticism, and the translation and analysis of the technical treatises on astronomy (*tianwen* 天文), topography (*dixing* 地形), and calendrics (*shize* 時則) by John S. Major in *Heaven and Earth in Early Han Thought: Chapters Three, Four, and Five of the Huainanzi* (1993), an interpretative work that does much to make good sense of Han dynasty cosmologies.

THE "SOURCE" IN *TRACING DAO TO ITS SOURCE*

The title of this treatise, "*Yuandao* 原道," means literally "to trace out *dao* and nourish one's life on this watery source."[6] It means to find the source of *dao* and to use it as a resource. The document opens with a statement of this image:

> As for *dao*: . . .
> Flowing from its source it becomes a gushing spring,
> What was empty slowly becomes full;
> First turbid and then surging forward,
> What was murky slowly becomes clear. (Section 1)

The *Shuowen* 說文 lexicon, which was compiled in the late first century AD, defines *yuan* 原 as *yuan* 源 or as the original form of this character, *yuan* 厵: "three springs under a cliff," making explicit the association between "source" and "water." It is significant that the notion of "source" appealed to here is natural rather than theological or metaphysical. *Yuan* is the continuing source or spring from which

13

things emerge and from which they draw their sustenance and nourishment. The language of "source" within the classical Daoist literature is ancestral and genealogical, often represented in specifically reproductive language: ancestor (*zong* 宗), mother (*mu* 母), fetal beginning (*shi* 始), gateway (*men* 門), predecessor of the ancestral emperor(s) (*di zhi xian* 帝之先), the vaginal opening of the mysterious female (*xuanpin zhi men* 玄牝之門), the female (*ci* 雌), the root of the world (*tiandi gen* 天地根), Heavenly ancestor(s) (*tian* 天), and so on. To find the source, then, is to trace out the course (*dao* 道) that has been trodden (*dao* 蹈) by those who have come before, the same path that gives us our bearings in the present moment.

In this particular document, placed at the beginning of the *Huainanzi*, the reflection on *dao* is abstract, often hyperbolic, and even mythological, challenging the reader's imagination as integral to its interpretation. Later treatises in this same text, then, are anecdotal and historical, recounting concrete incidents and personages that punctuate *dao* with remembered details of a shared human narrative.

The abstractness of this initial account of *dao* can be misleading. In the Daoist sense of "source," there is an important assumption that distinguishes it from what might be taken to be a similar pattern in classical Western metaphysics. That is, there is a possible equivocation between two very different senses of "cosmogony." We must distinguish a Daoist "world (*shijie* 世界)" that *emerges* genealogically—literally, "across the boundaries of successive generations"—from a "cosmos" or "universe" that is *derived* from some transcendent principle, a model familiar to us in classical Western accounts of origins. In the latter case, in what we might call a "metaphysical cosmogony," the originative and determinative principle stands independent of its creature—for example, the Judeo-Christian God or Plato's Forms—to impose a preassigned design on the chaos of a recalcitrant world. Natural change is instrumentalized, driven as it is by a linear teleology which takes us from creation to the realization of the given design. There is a plan, a beginning, a more or less straight line, and an end.

By contrast, the Daoist "genealogical cosmogony" is a notion of origins that is historicist, and, for the human being, biographical. It is an account of the narrative origins of a particular population as it has continued across time. But there is one question that arises unavoidably in the consideration of Daoist cosmogony. If non-Daoist cosmogony is usually an account of *initial* beginnings, in what sense is a resolutely genealogical cosmogony, which resists any absolute beginning, "cosmogonic"? Within the Daoist search for an explanation of origins, there is the assumption that the world is "self-so-ing (*ziran* 自然)" and autogenerative, with the energy of transformation residing within the process itself. There is no external efficient cause. Hence, there is no positing of initial beginnings; it is "turtles all the way down."

There is a second question that arises in the absence of an external efficient cause, a Creator. How do we distinguish a diachronic explanation of origins which focuses creativity in some initial beginning and the design that propels it—*creatio ex nihilo*—from a synchronic explanation of origins which describes the phenomenon of creation as it is being expressed broadly in this and every moment—that is, *creatio ab initio*?

Dao is nameless and formless. This is so because *dao* constitutes the noncoherent sum of all names and forms. As such, *dao* expresses both "one" and "many," both continuity and difference. The *Daodejing* 42 observes,

> *Dao* gives rise to one,
> One to two,
> Two to three,
> And three to the myriad things.
> The myriad things shoulder *yin* 陰 and embrace *yang* 陽 ,
> And mix the *qi* 氣 to achieve harmony.

An interpretative reading of this *Daodejing* chapter arguably within the tolerance of the language might be:

> *Dao* gives rise to continuity,
> Continuity to distinctions,
> Distinctions to plurality,
> And plurality to proliferation.

Our first impulse is to read this description diachronically as the proliferation of the many phenomena across time from some originative source. What encourages this interpretation is that it overlaps—sans originative principle—with metaphysical cosmogonies that are familiar in Western culture. In the language of *Daodejing* 25, this would be *dao* as "distance (*yuan* 遠)" and proliferation.

However, there is a less familiar and seldom rehearsed alternative understanding that is also part of an adequate explanation. We can also read this verse as a synchronic explanation of how in this very moment a simultaneous continuity gives rise to difference. On this second reading, given that the myriad transforming things in sum are constitutive of formless and nameless *dao*, we could just as well run the process back the other way with equal effect:

> The myriad things give rise to three,
> Three to two,
> Two to one,
> And one to *dao*.

In the language of Daoism, this is *dao* as "returning (*fan* 反)" and consolidation. Hence, the natural cosmology of classical China does not entail a single-ordered cosmos, but invokes an understanding of a dynamic "world" that is the sum of *dao*s construed by a myriad of unique particulars—"the ten thousand things." While from each perspective, *dao* as the context construed from that perspective is more or less coherent, *dao* as the sum of these contexts trades the coherence that would privilege one order among many, for continuity among them. *Dao* is, thus, the complex process of the world itself that does not reduce to any single order.

The water analogy that is so often evoked in explanation of *dao* is deliberate and provocative.[7] Is water one or many? Does water have a formal coherence that is persistent? Can water be meaningfully separated into "things," and if so, do such things persist? Is water noble, or is it base? Is it a thing ("water") or an action ("to water") or an attribute ("watery") or a modality ("fluidity")?

The water imagery of a "spring" or a "watery source" challenges any predilection we might have to overdetermine and reify the world around us. Water in many ways is a synecdoche for *qi* 氣, the sea of vital energy that is both constitutive of the world and an expression of its activities. Water is not only transformative, moving as it does from state to state, but at one moment it assumes the shape of its environment only to surrender its formal aspect in the next. This fluid and processional nature of water recalls a passage in *Zhuangzi*:

> With the ancients, understanding had gotten somewhere. Where was that? At its height, at its extreme, that understanding to which no more could be added was this: some of them thought that there had never begun to be things. The next lot thought that there are things, but that there had never begun to be boundaries among them. The next lot thought that there are boundaries among things, but that there had never begun to be right and wrong among them.[8]

Section 14 of *Tracing* Dao *to Its Source* is devoted explicitly to exploring and expanding upon the use of water as an analogy for *dao*, and in so doing, alludes to the *Daodejing*. Water is *yin-yang*: at once the weakest and the strongest of things, the most pliant and the hardest, the most nourishing and the most destructive, the most unselfish and the most self-inclined, the most insubstantial and the most concrete. Boundless, inexhaustible, formless, it circulates everywhere, and in being benefactor to everything from the highest to the lowest, it is not diminished in its own riches. Because of its contribution, it is described as the most exalted of all things—as "the supremely excellent (*zhide* 至德)."

Like *dao*, water is coterminous with and indistinguishable from the things that it nourishes: "it circulates and mingles, and has its beginning and end together with the myriad things." This is what is meant when the *Zhuangzi* observes that the path *is* the process of people walking it—the path is so because it is so:

> A path (*dao*) becomes a path by people walking it.
> A thing being called something becomes it.
> Why is it so?
> It is so because it is so.
> Why is it not something other than what it is?
> It is not because it is not.[9]

What recommends water as an explanatory analogy for *dao* is that it is *wuwei* 無爲 —literally, water does not purposely "do" anything, and yet the environment thrives because of its presence. In the Daoist tradition, the function of the sage, like water, is catalytic: to get the most out of the situation. This is another way of saying that each participant in the environment maintains its own integrity, while contributing itself fully and without reservation to its nexus of relationships. To accomplish this, the optimum disposition that must obtain among the various participants is one of deference, each allowing the others to be what they are. Coercion is anathema to this goal, and is seen as a wasteful diminution of available creative possibilities.

In *Tracing* Dao *to Its Source*, the sage is defined precisely in these noncoercive terms:

> Hence, the sage inwardly cultivates that which is the root instead of outwardly putting ornament on that which is the tip. He preserves his spirit and puts aside his cleverness. Quiescently he does nothing, yet leaves nothing undone; serenely he does not impose order on anything, yet there is nothing that is not ordered. By "doing nothing" is meant not being ahead of things in taking

18

action; by "leaving nothing undone" is meant making use of what is done by other things; by "not imposing order" is meant not putting in a substitute for what is so-of-itself; by "nothing not being properly ordered" is meant making use of the mutual recognition that obtains among things. (Section 11)

In similar passages in the text, "*dao*" and its surrogate, "water," stand in for "sage," celebrating this noncoercive relatedness as that disposition most conducive to a productive harmony (*he* 和).

"DAO" IN *TRACING DAO TO ITS SOURCE*

The absence of ontological assertions—assertions about a reality behind appearances—places the classical Chinese tradition in rather obvious contrast with the claim familiar among the classical Greek philosophers that there is some underlying substratum. For the early Chinese thinkers, there is no assumed "Being" behind the myriad beings, no "One" behind the many, no "Reality" behind appearance. Rather than the Parmenidean ontological *claim* that "Only *Being* is," there is the Daoist cosmological *project*, that is, to assure that "all of these becomings that are becoming do so efficaciously." There is no principle (*archē* > *principium*) of order—no superordinate One standing independent of the world to order it as an efficient cause. Rather, there is only the collaborative unfolding of the myriad things or events—the *wanwu* 萬物 or *wanyou* 萬有. Within this collaboration, there is an ever-changing processional regularity that can be discerned in the world around us, making experience *in some degree* coherent and determinate and, given its inherent indeterminacy, in some degree novel and unpredictable.

For classical India, there are many worlds of which this is one. For a Platonic Greece, there is one real world of which the world of sense and change is a poor reflection. The real world in its perfection is bounded, self-contained and self-sufficient, and is thus delimited and static. It is because the natural state of this reality is stasis that for

Aristotle a Prime Mover is a logical necessity. And it is the independence of *the* real world that provides a place from which to objectify it with definite articles such as "the" or "this." This ability to make an object of the world has allowed Western philosophers to decontextualize themselves and step out of the world in which they otherwise reside, thereby assuming a view from nowhere. And it is the absence of their subjectivity in this "view from nowhere" that guarantees the possibility of objective truth and certainty.

China is different. For classical China, neither dualistic like Greece nor pluralistic like India, there is *dao* or *ziran*: "world-as-such" or, better, just the perfective verbal noun "worlding" without the demonstrative pronoun "the" or "this" to objectify it. The Chinese "world-as-such" is unique, processional, and boundless, and the viewer is always resolutely and inextricably embedded within it.

THE PRIORITY OF SITUATION OVER AGENCY

In a world where the energy of change resides in the process itself without appeal to an external efficient cause, there can be little incentive to develop notions of discrete agency. If the world is the locus of change, the human situation which is played out in this world is the locus from which agency is derived. From the Chinese perspective, agents cannot be decontextualized and superordinated in any final sense; to identify and isolate an agent is an abstraction which removes it from the concrete reality of flux, exaggerating its continuity at the expense of its change. Since change is interior to all situations, human beings do not act upon a world that is independent of them. Rather, they are interdependent with the world in which they reside, simultaneously shaping it and being shaped by it. Order is always reflexive, entailing the agent within the action itself. Agency and action, subject and object, are not contraries, but interchangeable aspects of a single category in which any distinction between the agent and the action, between subject and object, between what does and what is done, is simply a matter of perspective.

The priority of situation over agency in the Chinese tradition is evident in this language of *dao* which does not require an external source of change. The Western understanding of human agency is based at least in part upon an analogy between the human being's real self, and Deity. In the Judeo-Christian tradition, God is the primary causal agent who exists independent of His creatures that are shaped by Him. Just as a unitary, perfect, and unchanging God originates activity and orders his creation purposefully, so unitary human beings as microcosm act from design to shape their world.

By contrast with this dominant Western model of order, classical Chinese philosophy has a fundamental commitment to process, to motion, to change. The classical Chinese language has no copula verb—no verb "to be"—and thus no impetus to join separate agents to their actions, persons to their contexts, or essences to their attributes. After all, it is the appeal to the copula verb—"He *is* Liu An"—that enables the language to separate agent from everything. Operating in the absence of the copula—"scholarly Liu An fell victim to Emperor Wu's clever scheming"—keeps the whole process together. Agent, action, attribute, and modality are all included in what is an event rather than a "thing." Thus, in classical China, a human being is not what one *is*; it is the compounding of what one *does*.

In the absence of a discrete and independent agent, "knowing" is the unraveling and the coordinating of the patterns of continuity that emerge and persist in the natural, social, and cultural flux around us. These patterned regularities give life coherence and make it more or less predictable. The continuities are not imposed upon the world by some external agency; rather, they reside within the world as the rhythm and cadence symptomatic of a living stream. And the human being is simply one impulse integral to this continually unfolding process.

The essentializing model of order invests a great deal in causal explanations that attempt to identify and isolate the discrete agent responsible for an event, while the Chinese model is situational, seeking to understand the whole range of relevant causal conditions and the relations that obtain among them as they come to sponsor any given occurrence.

The classical Western search for order is ambitious; its goal is the clear, the exact, the comprehensive knowledge of the unitary cosmic design and the forces that drive it—those natural and moral "laws" that structure and regulate the natural and human universe. The Chinese approach is more modest; it seeks to understand the continuities that define and give meaning to *this* particular moment and *this* particular place in life's ongoing process.

The "two-world" model is based on the concept of a universal blueprint made up of unchanging formal patterns which, once understood, make change predictable and logarithmic, reducible to a given pattern. The "one-world" Chinese model allows that regularity is always attended by change, making order always dynamic, site-specific, and provisional. Given that the patterned regularity is never decontextualized nor detemporalized, the rhythm of life is indefatigable and irreversible, and is evident in the configuration of each snowflake, the grain of each piece of wood, the aura of each sunset, the complexity of each personality, as these always-unique phenomena emerge in the temporal flow only to recede into it again. Because the Chinese order entails a thoroughly symbiotic relationship between its formal and its fluid aspects, every situation is necessarily unique, making globalizing and essentializing generalizations problematic.

DAO AS "THE ONENESS OF THINGS"

Tracing Dao *to Its Source* follows the other Daoist texts in associating *dao* with "the oneness of things." But, as we have suggested, this is not to surrender the particularity of things, dissolving them into some unitary and perfect whole. Rather, it is a recognition that each and every unique phenomenon is continuous with every other phenomenon within its field of experience, and its field of experience is again continuous with every other field of experience. Because the world is processional and because its creativity is *ab initio* rather than *ex nihilo*—a creativity expressed across the careers of its constitutive phenomena as opposed to being invested by some independent source—its patterned regularity and its content are always provisional and under construction. Phenomena are never either atomistically discrete nor complete. As *Tracing Dao to Its Source* observes,

> Hence, when the "one" is disentangled
> It can be dealt out to the four seas,
> And when the "one" is unraveled
> It will reach the limits of heaven and earth. . . .
> The convergence of the myriad things
> Goes through a single aperture;
> The roots of the various happenings
> All issue forth from a single gateway.
> Its movements are hidden from sight
> And its changes and transformations are godlike;
> It does not leave any traces behind in its progress;
> It is ever in the lead though always coming behind. (Section 15)

It is at this point that the applicability of the very word "cosmology," at least in its familiar classical Greek sense, becomes problematic. In pre-Socratic philosophy, the term "*kosmos*" connotes a clustered range of meanings, including *archē* (originative, material, and efficient cause/ultimate undemonstrable principle), *logos* (underlying organizational principle), *theoria* (contemplation), *nomos* (law), *theios* (divinity), *nous* (intelligibility). In combination, this cluster of terms conjures forth some notion of a single-ordered divine[10] universe governed by natural and moral laws ultimately intelligible to the human mind.

However, this "*kosmos*" terminology meaning "a single-ordered world" is culturally specific. The notion of "one" is ambiguous. It can mean one-of-a-*kind*, such as one member of a set of things, or *one*-of-a-kind, such as a unique, inimitable work of art. In classical Western "one-many" metaphysics, this equivocation between "one" and "unique" is resolved in favor of "one," thereby disqualifying the possibility of anything being "unique." In any of the various conceptions of a single-ordered universe assumed by the early systematic philosophers wherein the many phenomena reduce to some One, all phenomena are identical with respect to their dependence upon this One as their determinative source. In a Judeo-Christian universe, for example, all phenomena are identical in the sense that they are dependent upon and explicable by reference to a transcendent creator deity.

In classical Chinese reflections on world order, the equivocation between "one" and "unique" is resolved in favor of uniqueness. Each particular phenomenon is unique, and the field of experience as it is entertained from each of these vantage points is also unique. As the incoherent sum of all orders, the nameless and formless *dao* gives rise to "one" as "continuity," and entailed in this continuity is an always proliferating difference. The point is that the natural cosmology of classical China is not a single-ordered cosmos that returns its many phenomena to a superordinated and independent One; it is a cosmos in which the unique many are constitutive of the ever unique, ever changing, and thus, ever unbounded *dao*.

What encourages us in the shadow of the Western metaphysical tradition to separate time and space is our inclination inherited from the Greeks to see things in the world as fixed in their formal aspect, and thus, as bounded and limited. Instead of giving ontological privilege to the formal aspect of phenomena, the Chinese were inclined to observe them in light of their ceaseless transformation. Temporalizing phenomena and thus perceiving them as "events" rather than "things," they took each phenomenon-in-process to be entirely real. In fact, the pervasive capacity of the manifest world to transform continuously *is* the meaning of time.

The Chinese binomial most frequently translated as *kosmos* is *yuzhou* 宇宙, a term that overtly expresses not simply the interdependence of space and time, but their mutuality. *Yu* refers literally to the "eaves," and by extension, "boundary, territory." *Zhou* is the "moving canopy," and hence "duration." *Kosmos* (*yuzhou*) is defined in the *Zhuangzi* as:

> That which is tangible (*shi* 實), yet has no place in which it dwells, is *yu*; enduring (*chang* 常), yet having neither root nor tip to it, is *zhou*.[11]

"Things" dwell in places; only *tangibility*, which reduces neither to thing nor place, is the stuff of the world. "Things" dwell in time; the *persistence* of tangibility, which reduces neither to thing nor place without beginning or end, is time.

For China, and again in contrast with the dominant impulse of Greece and India, time pervades everything and is not to be denied; it is not derivative of tangibility, but a fundamental aspect of it. Unlike traditions which devalue time and change in pursuit of the timeless and eternal, in classical China, things are by nature always transforming (*wuhua* 物化).

As we have seen, in the *Daodejing* 25, *dao* is described in terms of "distance (*yuan* 遠)" as the particular becomes increasingly distinguished, and "return (*fan* 反)" as the same particular continues to participate in the "transformation of things (*wuhua* 物化)," relinquishing its present perspective and its construal of its field (*dao*), only to be resolved into other things. The particular focus (*de*) and its field (*dao*) are thus a dynamic continuum which can be expressed in this language of distance and return.

Since there is nothing which is not *dao*, there is no external standard against which it can be measured or corrected. This then is the meaning of the phrase, "standing alone it is not reformed (*gai* 改)." That *dao* is unique, however, does not preclude the fact that it is processional (*shi* 逝), and constantly changing.[12]

Metaphysical cosmogony is very ambitious: it attempts to trace the "many" back to the ordering and determinative One. For Aristotle, *episteme* is the knowledge of the causes of being, and the knowledge of the ultimate causes is the highest level of *episteme*, wisdom. Under the light of such wisdom, all becomes intelligible.

If, as in the Chinese alternative, order is emergent rather than existing as an independent scientific principle, knowledge of it must be qualified by the where and the when of it. As such, knowledge must be provisional, and more modest in its claims. The Daoist cosmogonic narrative takes us back to an earlier set of conditions which, as they recede from us historically, offer increasing resistance to explanation by the application of our present philosophical vocabulary. The various aspects of emergent *dao* and our strategies for organizing and understanding it—*yin* and *yang*, time and space, heaven and earth, *qi*, the five phases (*wuxing* 五行)— must be historicized as a contingent vocabulary for the world order as we know it here and now. Thus, to the extent that *episteme* can be rehabilitated to fit the classical Chinese worldview, the cosmogonic narrative is also an "epistegonic" account which provides an emerging understanding of world order. Importantly, at the same time, this account sets historical limits on our understanding. Our relatively clear understanding of our present situation cannot be "universalized" and relied upon to explain all past or future situations. These categories cannot stand as "principles"—as objective, necessary, a priori conditions that locate us within a Greek "universe."

There is another aspect of "knowing" *dao* that wants clarification. In classical Western epistemology, *episteme* refers to a particular kind of knowledge: true, necessary, and demonstrable knowledge. For Plato, for example, the objects of such knowledge are the *eide* or Forms. When we turn to the classical Chinese tradition, we find that there is no distinction between knowledge and wisdom. Knowing is always practical, contingent, and moral: it is a "doing" rather than a state of mind. Further, "knowing" is meliorative—it makes a situation better. "Knowing" is thus more pragmatic than theoretical. While certainly not a kind of *metis* or "cunning" because of the moral paucity of such knowledge, it still is a task- or proficiency-based awareness which, when fortified by imagination, enables one to move one's project ahead. Such knowing gives rise to creative strategies that enable one to be efficacious in what one does.

Given the inseparability of agent and context assumed in this tradition, *dao* has as much to do with the subjects of knowing and their quality of understanding as it does with any object of knowledge. Without an originative principle, and the linear teleology that comes with it, the world has no persisting governing purpose, and no preassigned design. The alternative to some given and governing purpose, then, is localized and temporalized self-sufficiency—a collaboration between the human knower and the world as it is realized, to get the most out of each situation. Thus, "knowing" *dao* is always proximate—you have to be there.

THE GERUNDICAL *DAO*

The parts of speech inherent in our Western languages—subjects and predicates, nouns, verbs, adjectives, and adverbs—encourage us to divide up the world in a given, culturally specific way. Under the influence of the "deep structure" of both our syntax and our semantics, we are inclined to separate things from actions, attributes from modalities, the where from the when, and the why or how from the what—all of these according to foundational Aristotelian categories. However, these categories which Aristotle took to be basic features of reality do not govern the way in which the Chinese world is divided up. In fact, categories used to define a Chinese world are fluid, and must be seen as often crossing the borders of time, space, and matter in an unfamiliar way. *Dao* so understood offends against the most basic of Western cultural distinctions, mixing together subject and object, as well as things, actions, attributes, and modalities. *Dao* is at once "what is" (things and their attributes) and "how things are" (actions and their modalities), it is "who knows" as well as "what is known."

THE CONTINUITY OF *DAO* AND THE HUMAN WORLD

There are consequences for insisting upon "the continuity of things." For example, without the assumption that one can stand outside of the world to assert objective truths, the line between description and prescription blurs because subjects are always reflexively implicated in the way in which they organize the world. To say something about the world is to say something about themselves. Their choices, values, and cultural importances are implicit in their interpretations of experience.

The structure and organization of the *Huainanzi* is itself an apt illustration of the inseparability of fact and human values. We might locate the first two treatises of the text somewhere between *mythos* and *historia*: the story of origins told through images, rich in metaphor and other such rhetorical tropes. The following three treatises, by contrast, tend towards *logos*: the "technical" discussions of astronomy, topography, and calendrics respectively. However, as we have stated, the absence of a basis for making objective statements about the world makes fact and value interdependent and mutually entailing. Objective definitions and simple descriptions are thus problematic. The values of the observer are invariably implicated in the observation. The line, then, that would separate science from the arts—chemistry from alchemy, astronomy from astrology, geology from geomancy, psychology from physiognomy, medicine from hygienics, kinesiology from recreative play, and so on—is always porous.

Another consequence of operating without reference to an objective perspective is that *saying* and even *thinking* something about the world is *doing* something to it. The severe separation between theory and practice that makes "thinking" and "speaking" separate from "doing" is dependent upon the possibility that what is "theoretical" does not change the world. In the classical Chinese worldview and even in the Chinese world today, thinking and speaking are perceived as "actions" that have real consequences in shaping our environments.

THE RELATIONSHIP BETWEEN "HEAVEN" AND "HUMANITY"

Zhang Dongsun 張東蓀 is a comparative philosopher who seems to have come a generation or two before his time. In trying to identify and respect some uncommon assumptions that separate the Chinese tradition from the West, he observes:

> These two kinds of thinking not only differ in terms of categories and the value of their terms, but also differ markedly in their attitudes. If we take inquiry, for example, Western thinking, in respect of any particular thing or event, is inclined to ask "What is it?" before asking "How do we deal with it?" Chinese thinking, on the other hand, is inclined to do the opposite: "How do we deal with it?" takes precedence. Thus I would say that the West has a "*what* priority attitude" while China has a "*how* priority attitude."[13]

Said another way, this means that the focus of classical Chinese philosophy is cosmology rather than ontology: "knowing *how* the world should hang together" rather than "knowing *what* the reality is behind appearances." It is the construction of a way of living (*dao*) that we can trust, rather than the pursuit of the truth. Hence, one of the defining questions during the formative period of Chinese culture is "*How* should we construe the relationship between Heaven (*tian* 天) and humanity (*ren* 人), between the natural and the human worlds?" The pervasive answer to this question found in the classical corpus, although complex and multivalent, is perhaps best summed up in the assumption that there is "a continuity between Heaven and humanity (*tianren heyi* 天人合一)." In order to understand the position advanced in this particular Daoist treatise, *Tracing* Dao *to Its Source*, we need to locate it within the philosophical narrative of the late Zhou and early Han.

For Confucius the continuity between Heaven (or more literally, "sky") and man, following in the Zhou tradition, is familial—*tian* is perceived as the ancestral progenitor of human beings. This hierarchical familial relationship between *tian* and humanity is made explicit politically in the expression, "the son of *tian* (*tianzi* 天子)," deemed an appropriate title for the ruler of humanity. Predictably, the same vocabulary is used to characterize order in both the human and the natural worlds. *Wen* 文 is both human culture (*wenhua* 文化) and astronomy/astrology as "the pattern of the skies (*tianwen* 天文)"; *li* 理 is both "the structure of the human heart-and-mind (*xinli* 心理)" and "the structure of the physical world (*wuli* 物理)"; *dao* is both "the way of living for the human being (*rendao* 人道)" and "the workings of nature (*tiandao* 天道)."

The identification of the high ancestors of a human population with "the sky," collapsing categories that usually separate the human world from natural phenomena, reflects an understanding of the notion of *qi* 氣, "vital energy," that is an unannounced assumption in Chinese cosmology. That is, the most dense and coarse *qi* constitutes the lowest and least animate phenomena, the earthly physical world, while the most rarified and subtle *qi* makes up the most noble and animated aspects of the world, the more celestial human beings and the ancestral spirits.

CONFUCIANISM AND THE CONTINUITY
BETWEEN HEAVEN AND HUMANITY

For Confucius, at once profoundly religious and profoundly human-centered, spirituality is to be expressed through the quality of interpersonal continuities that constitute a flourishing community. Just as participating in a robust family life is "governing" the world,[14] so deferring to one's parents as a filial son is an expression of religious piety.[15] While adamant that sacrifices be carried out with the utmost solemnity and genuineness,[16] Confucius still wants the locus of religious experience to be here and now in the human community rather than piety directed towards some transcendent "Other" residing at the dark limits of our understanding.[17]

But it was Xunzi, the most prominant and influential Confucian of his time, who really set the terms for the debate over the appropriate relationship between *tian* and humanity. Because of Xunzi's early rise to fame at the Jixia Academy in the powerful state of Qi, it is his voice that echoes through the literature of this period. His naturalistic position on the appropriate relationship between Heaven and humanity is in many respects close to that of Confucius. He sees *tian* as the regular natural processes which make human life possible, but which at the same time are totally indifferent to human prosperity and adversity. For Xunzi, human morality is the product of concerted human effort. It consists of conventions laid down by wise people of antiquity and passed on generation after generation. Consistent with his naturalism, Xunzi avers teleological and supernatural explanations for natural events. Further, he encourages a clear distinction between what is natural and what is human. While advocating the full exploitation of *tian* as an available resource, at the same time he insists that human beings concentrate their efforts on the human world, and leave the working of *tian* to *tian* itself. Succinctly put,

> The greatest cleverness lies in what is not done and the greatest wisdom lies in what is not thought about. . . . Thus, if people abandon the affairs of the human being to conjecture on the business of *tian*, they will lose sight of the real circumstances of those things around them.[18]

Enter Zhuangzi, a rival of Xunzi at the Jixia Academy. As A. C. Graham has pointed out,[19] Zhuangzi begins his reflection on the appropriate relationship between Heaven and humanity by rehearsing a popular position of the day—in fact, he is summarizing Xunzi's position:

> To know what Heaven does and to know what the human being does is the height of knowledge. Knowing what Heaven does is produced by Heaven itself. To know what the human being does is to use the knowledge one has to develop knowledge that one does not have. To live out one's natural span of years without dying prematurely—this is an abundance of knowledge.

Zhuangzi then takes exception to this dichotomous position, pointing out what he takes to be two fatal flaws:

> But there are some difficulties with this proposition. First, knowing is only confirmed when there is evidence for it, yet what counts as evidence has never been fixed. How do we know that what we are calling "Heaven" is not "human," and vice versa? And secondly, there must be an authentic person (zhenren 眞人) before there can be authentic knowing (zhenzhi 眞知).

The starting point for Zhuangzi in this critique of Xunzi is that "knowing" is relational, and hence Heaven and the human world cannot be separated.

On the classical Western side, a familiar conception of truth is a correspondence between *what* is real—the Being behind the beings, and *what* is representational—a mental mirroring of what really is. On the Chinese side, with its "how-priority attitude," the ambition is of a different order. With no separation between phenomena and ontological foundations, "reality" is precisely that complex pattern of relationships which in sum constitute the myriad things of the world. Knowledge, then, is not abstract, but concrete; it is not representational, but performative and participatory; it involves, not closure, but disclosure; it is not discursive, but is, rather, a specific kind of know-how: how to effect robust and productive relationships.

Again we see the importance of this "how-priority" thinking of the classical Chinese cited by Zhang Dongsun earlier. This peculiar orientation to the "How?" question has the broadest of possible effects on the Chinese manner of thinking. To cite Zhang Dongsun on *tian* specifically:

> The Chinese attitude toward the demands of *tian* are only to know its purposes in order to secure good fortune and avoid misfortune. As to what kind of thing *tian* is, they are indifferent. This is because the Chinese people do not use the category of ontology with respect to *tian*, and do not consider it to be the ontological ground of the myriad things.[20]

It is certainly the case that notions such as *tian* are profoundly recondite in the Chinese classics, with language such as "distant (*yuan* 遠)" and "dark (*xuan* 玄)" being frequently invoked to describe it. This is because the project in a text such as the *Analects* is not to speculate on *what* the ultimate source of value in the world might be, but to recount *how* one sensitive man—Confucius—made his way in the world as a possible model for others. The *Daodejing* does not purport to provide an adequate and compelling description of *what dao* and *de* might mean as an ontological explanation for the world around us; rather, it seeks to engage us and to provide guidance in *how* we *ought* to interact with the phenomena, human and otherwise, that give us context in the world. And the *Book of Changes* is not a systematic cosmology that seeks to explain the sum of all possible situations we might encounter in order to provide insight into what to do, but is a resource providing a vocabulary of images that enable us to think through and articulate an appropriate response to the changing conditions of our lives.

"Knowing," then, in classical Daoism is not so much a knowing *what*, which provides some understanding of the environing conditions of the natural world, but is rather a knowing *how* to be adept in our relationships, and *how*, in optimizing the possibilities that these relations provide, to develop a sense of trust in their viability. The cluster

33

of terms that define knowing are thus programmatic and exhortative, encouraging as they do the quality of the roles and associations that define us. Propositions may be true, but it is more important that husbands and friends, and in fact, all of the relations which bind us into our social, cultural, and natural environments, be so.

Rather than a vocabulary of truth and falsity, right and wrong, good and evil—terms that speak to the "whatness" of things—we find pervasively the language of harmony and disorder, genuineness and hypocrisy, trust and dissimulation, adeptness and ineptness—terms which reflect the priority of the continuity that obtains among things: "how well" things hang together.

Given that the heart-and-mind (*xin* 心) does the work of both cognizing and feeling, there is no dichotomous relationship between intellection and sensation, between thinking and living. This point can be reinforced by rehearsing what Zhang Dongsun takes to be the distinguishing characteristics of Chinese epistemology. When the knower and the known establish a relationship, according to Zhang, there are three conditions:

> i) they are intrinsically related such that each relationship influences the other, the relationships are intricate and complex, and each member of the relationship is different after the relationship has been established, and changes with it;
> ii) all relationships are mediated by layer after layer of intervening experience, rather than being unmediated and direct;
> iii) and knowledge is always a kind of interpretation rather than a copy or representation.

In Zhang Dongsun's characterization of Chinese epistemology, we would have to allow that he is not only reflecting on epistemic assumptions characteristic of the Chinese tradition, but more fundamentally and importantly, on ethics: that is, how personal, communal, and political relationships are formed and develop. The epistemic commitment lies in "realizing" a viable community rather than "knowing" the truth about the world.

One might want to argue, as Xunzi does, that the Daoists do maintain a distinction between the human and the natural world by siding with the natural against the human. This was his specific complaint against Zhuangzi:

> Zhuangzi was blinkered by *tian*, and did not know humanity.[21]

Certainly there are passages in the *Zhuangzi* that would suggest this:

> The authentic person (*zhenren*) of antiquity did not know pleasure for life nor displeasure for death. He embarked on life without rejoicing and passed on without resistance. Like a flash he came; like a flash he went, and that was all. . . . This is what is called not aiding *dao* with our minds, and not assisting *tian* with the human.[22]

But to give Zhuangzi his best argument, we would have to allow that he was fully aware that this human/not-human dichotomy is problematic, and that his compensatory efforts to reinstate the natural were not an advocacy of the natural at the expense of the human. In fact, the *Zhuangzi* criticizes the Confucian for buying into such a distinction, and being preoccupied with the human world:

> The house of Youyu (that is, the "Confucian" sage, Shun) is no match for the House of Tai (the patriarch of the Daoist "Ultimate" clan). Youyu still hung onto *ren* 仁 in order to intercept other people, and even though he was indeed able to win them over, he never made his way out into what was not-human (*feiren* 非人). As for Tai, he would sleep deeply and contentedly, and would take on the perspective of a horse and sometimes a cow. In his awareness he was sensitive and confident, his *de* was utterly genuine (*zhen* 眞), and he never began to enter into what was not-human (*feiren* 非人).[23]

In this passage, the Confucian does not venture out into what is not-human (*feiren*) because of his exclusive commitment to the human world. The Daoist has never entered into what is not-human (*feiren*) because, dealing with *dao* indiscriminately, he does not entertain a human/not-human distinction.

In fact, as we have seen above, Zhuangzi says flatly,

> How do we know that what we are calling "Heaven" is not "human," and vice versa?

The *Zhuangzi* proposes its resolution to this dichotomy between Heaven and man, between nature and the human world, in its description of the Daoist "intact person (*quanren* 全人)." First, it reiterates Xunzi's criticism of Zhuangzi:

> Yi the archer was skilled at hitting minute targets but clumsy at preventing others from making him celebrated because of it. The sage is skilled at what is natural but clumsy at what is human.

Then it offers the alternative that trumps this lopsided "sage":

> To be skilled at what is natural and to be equally good at what is human—only the intact person (*quanren*) can do this! Only insects can be both insects and be natural. The complete person hates what is natural, and hates what is natural about what is human. How much more does he hate this flip-flopping between "Am I natural?" or "Am I human?"[24]

TRACING DAO TO ITS SOURCE AND THE CONTINUITY BETWEEN HEAVEN AND HUMANITY

On a first reading, *Tracing Dao to Its Source* seems to accept the distinction between *tian* and man, siding with Heaven against the human:

> By "Heaven" is meant
>> Pure and unadulterated like uncarved wood and undyed silk,
>> Original simplicity and sheer whiteness,
>> Which has never been admixed with anything else.
> By "man" is meant
>> Studying each other and exercising one's knowledge and
>> presuppositions,

Being crafty and deceptive to others,
In order to get on in the world
And to be able to deal with the vulgar.

Thus, an ox's having cloven hoofs and horns,
And a horse's having a mane and uncloven hoofs
Is what is "Heaven";
Bridling a horse's mouth
And boring an ox's nose
Is "man."
Those who follow Heaven ramble about with *dao*,
Whereas those who accede to man have dealings with the
vulgar. (Section 10)

But this passage is in fact borrowed from the *Zhuangzi*, and as with
the *Zhuangzi*, the assumption that this text sides with Heaven against
man is not borne out. In fact, the primary concern is for human beings
to maintain their own integrity without agitating their natural equanimity with unwanted distractions:

Thus, one who understands *dao*
Does not barter what belongs to Heaven for what is man's.
While externally he is transformed along with the transfor-
mation of things,
Internally he does not become other than what he is really
like. (Section 5)

The category "Heaven" here is both "inner" and "outer," including
both the natural world and those natural conditions which are defining
of human integrity. "Man," on the other hand, refers to the unnatural
preoccupations which disturb both the person and the environment.
The point here is that "integrity" is not genetic, but achieved within
one's context, and for one to lose one's integrity is to jeopardize the
integrity of one's natural, social, and cultural environments. On the
other hand, persons who preserve their integrity wander contentedly
through the world as companions with the processes of change:

Thus, the sage does not adulterate Heaven with man,
>
> And does not allow desire to disturb his actual nature.
>
> He hits the mark without planning,
>
> His word is trusted without his having to speak,
>
> He succeeds without deliberating,
>
> He accomplishes without doing.
>
> His purity reaches up to the mansion of the spirits
>
> And he is a comrade of the demiurge of change. (Section 10)

SEIZING THE MOMENT

What is the role of the human being in the unfolding of *dao*? In China, the pursuit of wisdom has perennially centered on finding a way to stabilize, to discipline, and to shape productively and elegantly the unstoppable stream of change in which the human experience is played out. Given the always unique and always provisional nature of *dao*—a work in progress, as it were—the human being has and continues to have a creative part in forging the path.

The term *dao* (道) combines in itself continuity, novelty, and an indeterminate leading edge (*dao* 導) that allows for effective manipulation. Often, the most advantageous position for leading—for "seizing the moment"—is from behind.

> By "coming behind" is not meant being stagnant, numb, and inert. Rather, it means putting store in always being in accord with that which is necessarily so, and being appropriate to the moment. When a person grasps the principles of *dao* and uses them to match change, then he controls others whether he is in the lead or in the rear. Why is this? Because he does not let go of the means to control others, giving others no chance of controlling him.
>
> (Section 12)

"Seizing the moment" is a particularly appropriate expression because, given the processional nature of *dao* and its propensity to unfold in this direction as opposed to that, proper timing is essential:

38

The right moment becomes the wrong
Before one can take a breath.
One who acts too soon anticipates the opportunity,
And one who acts too late gets left behind.
The sun revolves, the moon wheels its course,
And the right moment waits for no man.
Thus, the sage values an inch of time over a foot of precious jade.
It is because the right moment is so hard to catch and so easy to miss.

(Section 13)

As well as underscoring the importance of timing, "moment" gives us the situatedness and the cognate associations that we need to probe the meaning of *dao*. "Moment" at once entails "momentum" in the sense of the ineluctable propensity of things, "motive" in the sense of directedness and goal, "the right moment" in the sense of timing, "emotion" in the sense of motive force, and "momentous" in the sense of importance.

The most pervasive image of this moving line in the philosophical literature is the one, cumulative path (*dao*)—the continuous moving line of culture that is under construction by the "roadbuilders" of each generation. This moving line, defining the ever changing, ever provisional, cultural horizon, has many images: in calligraphy and painting, it is captured in the brush stroke (*yihua* 一畫), in art and ornamentation, it is expressed as the fabulous dragon (*long* 龍) and phoenix (*fenghuang* 鳳凰), in poetry, it is the measured cadence of each line, in the art of warfare, it is the formulation and manipulation of strategic advantage (*shi* 勢). Importantly, the shaping of this moving line as it inscribes the cultural tradition is an art and an achievement.

Appreciating the energy inherent in and expressed by the moving line, the contemporary scholar Li Zehou develops an interesting analogy between the art of the line in design and calligraphy, and the rhythm and harmonies expressed in everything from musical composition to architecture. He draws a contrast between the nature of "formal beauty" on the one hand, which is standardized, static, and stylized, and the "significant form" inscribed by the line—vigorous, animated, and beautiful in its allusions to life.[25]

Understanding, handling, and maneuvering the moving line to achieve harmony requires a full consideration of both determinate and indeterminate forces, for each situation is unique, and is thus inevitably attended by a certain degree of unpredictability. This sense of underdeterminacy within order is expressed in the Chinese language itself.

A pair of recurring terms that reflect this ubiquitous indeterminate aspect is *ji* 幾 and its homophonous cognate, *ji* 機, both having a rather curious semantic range when rendered into a European language. *Ji* 幾 begins from the notion of "first inklings or stirrings," "minute," "imminent," "nearly," and then extends to "probability," "anticipation," "occasion," and with *ji* 機 it extends yet further to "critical point," "turning point," "pivot," "danger," and hence to "impetus," "motive force," "trigger," "clever device." Finally, *ji* 機 means "opportunity," and, describing the person who is able to seize the opportunity, "adroit," "flexible," "ingenious."

What is the sense of order expressed in this seemingly broad range of meanings? In the articulation of any situation, the indeterminate aspect is usually "small"—a "first stirring"—which, as a "moving force" for self-reorganization and reconstrual, becomes its "critical turning point (*weiji* 危機)." There is an appreciation of how, in complex natural processes, small alterations can produce scale-variant cascading effects. As a critical turning point, this inchoate, indeterminate aspect can literally be either a "danger (*wei* 危)" or an "opportunity (*ji* 機)," depending on whether or not one is "adroit" in being able to seize the moment and make the most of it.

This term *ji* 幾 —with its seamless range of meanings—occurs in those canonical documents that have defined the classical Chinese worldview. For example, the "Great Treatise" of the *Book of Changes* (*Yijing*) associates *ji* 幾 with "deep and profound (*shen* 深)" and "spiritual, mysterious, inscrutable (*shen* 神)":

The *Book of Changes* is the sage's way of probing what is profound to its limit, and of getting to the very gist of things (*ji* 幾). It is only through this profundity that the sage can come to understand the propensities of the world; it is only through its pivotal significance (*ji* 幾) that he can be successful in the business of the world; it is only through its mystery that he can be quick without haste and can arrive without going.[26]

Tracing Dao *to Its Source* concludes on a similar note: the sage is able to ride *dao* and function effectively as a collaborator with the natural processes by keeping his finger on the trigger (*ji* 機):

> Hence, the sage nurtures his spirit, harmonizes and retains the fluency of his *qi*, calms his body, and sinks and floats, rises and falls with dao.
>
> > Placidly, giving it its head,
> > When borne down upon, he makes use of it.
> > When he gives it its head, it is like shedding a coat;
> > In using it, it is like touching off a trigger. (Section 22)

RIDING THE DRAGON (*LONG* 龍)

This image of "seizing the moment" to achieve productive harmony (*he* 和) is constructed in different ways in *Tracing* Dao *to Its Source*. In Section 2, Tai Huang ("Greatly August") and Gu Huang ("Anciently August")—that is, both space and temporality—stand at the center and work the handle of *dao*, offering a variation on the "trigger" image and producing not only a human world that is socially and politically stable, but a natural world that is ecologically sound. In such a world, the cadence of life and death achieves its proper rhythm and balance.

> > Their *de* embraced the heavens and the earth and brought
> > > harmony to the *yin* and the *yang*,
> > Ordered the four seasons and regulated the five phases.
> > > Brooding over things and nurturing them,
> > > The myriad things in all of their variety were produced.

41

> They provided moistening nourishment to the
>   grasses and trees
> And penetrated the minerals and rocks.
> The birds and beasts grew large and tall
> With coats glossy and sleek,
> Wings sprouting out and horns growing, animals did not
> miscarry and birds did not lay addled eggs, fathers were spared
> the suffering of mourning their sons and elder brothers were
> spared the grief of weeping over the younger ones,
> Children were not orphaned
> Nor were wives widowed,
> Evil confluences of the *yin* and the *yang* did not
>   appear
> Nor did ominous celestial portents occur. (Section 2)

The image of the control handles and the chariot come together in the master charioteer who gallops to the far ends of the world to pass through the gates of Heaven. In the Daoist tradition, the opening and the closing of these gates is symbolic of the process of change itself:

> Hence, he [the man of great stature] travels fast without pitching
> And travels far without fatigue.
> Without taxing his four limbs,
> And without draining the keenness of his hearing and sight,
> He knows the lay and the boundaries of the various divisions
> and quadrants of the cosmos. How is this so? It is because he has
> his hands on the control handles of *dao* and rambles in the land
> of the inexhaustible. (Section 4)

In Section 4, the legendary drivers Ping Yi and Da Bing harness the cloud dragons to their thunder chariot and streak across the horizon. Skillful charioting—finding one's way—is an epistemic image. "Knowing" *dao* is being able to lead the myriad things to realize a world of relationships that is free of power and coercion. Climbing the skies and coursing through the cosmos requires collaboration and sensitivity, sometimes galloping the team and sometimes dismounting to walk the dragons through a difficult patch. It is not where you are going, but how you get there, that is telling of the superlative charioteer.

The *long* 龍 —unfortunately translated into English as "dragon," a serpentine animal that, in Western mythology, is properly slain—is a pervasive, usually positive icon in the Chinese tradition.[27] It is yet another way of "imaging" the moving line. Now undulating, sprawling, wriggling, coiling, spiraling, thrusting, and ultimately soaring through the clouds, this "every animal" captures the notion of unrestricted transformation and articulation (*wenhua* 文化) across the axes of time, space, and light.

Where does the *long* as an emblem of changing cultural horizons begin in the Chinese tradition? *Long* is an image that has dominated Chinese cosmology from ancient times. Fu Xi 伏羲 and Nü Wa 女媧, the high ancestors who are credited with developing the fundaments of Chinese culture such as farming, fishing, and abstract symbols (the eight diagrams), are described and represented in the earliest texts as human figures with the bodies of snakes. In fact, this representation is typical of many of the gods, supernaturals, and cultural heroes that are remembered in ancient Chinese legends. Over time, this snakelike figure, now swallowing creatures whole, now shedding its skin, accumulated the features of "every animal" to become the generative and transformative symbol of Chinese culture—the totemic Chinese *long*. This emblem is not only pervasive in the mythology of China, but is everywhere in the natural landscape and architecture of the country. Unquestionably the most substantial presentation of the *long* imagery is the Great Wall, composite of many walls, as it peaks and lunges, dances and glides, meandering across thousands of miles and countless generations to give expression to the cadence of time as much as to space.

Tu Wei-ming sees this *long* as a symbol of the process of accumulation and integration that occurred in the proto-Chinese world, where disparate tribes with disparate emblems of identity combined their resources:

As a composite totem, the dragon possesses at least the head of a tiger, the horns of a ram, the body of a snake, the claws of an eagle and the scales of a fish. Its ability to cross totemic boundaries and its lack of verisimilitude to any living creature strongly suggest that from the very beginning the dragon was a deliberate cultural construction. The danger of anachronism notwithstanding, the modern Chinese ethnic self-definition as the "dragon race" indicates a deep-rooted sense that Chineseness may derive from many sources.[28]

Significantly, the expression *zhongguo* 中國 , going back to the Spring and Autumn period (722–481 BCE), is properly understood not as the singular "Middle Kingdom," but as the "Central Kingdoms"—the diverse states that together made up the world of Zhou China. Similarly, the *long* icon stretches back across history to represent fluidity, diversity and inclusivity—the porousness and absorbency of the Chinese polity and its culture.

STILLING THE HEART-AND-MIND (*XIN* 心)

"Riding the dragon" requires a fluid responsiveness between the driver and his steeds, between the chariot and the way. Above we saw that water with its various characteristics is frequently evoked as an analogy for *dao*. With respect to "knowing the way," we find that this analogy between water and *dao* is extended in yet another way—that is, in the capacity of water to mirror the world as it is manifest, without imposing presuppositions and values upon it:

> It is because the mirror and water do not, in anticipation, equip themselves with cleverness, that the shapes they come into contact with cannot but show themselves as they are: square, round, bent and straight. Hence, an echo does not resound as it likes, and a shadow is not something that is cast once and for all. The likeness of the sound and shape is attained without fuss.
>
> (Section 5)

Tracing Dao *to Its Source* suggests that the optimum posture of the human heart-and-mind (*xin* 心), like water and the mirror, is to achieve and maintain that degree of equanimity which will enable it to take in the world as it is without imposing its own values upon it, and without allowing the world to cause it agitation.

First we must distinguish this "mirroring" metaphor from how it has been understood within the Western philosophical tradition because, given the central importance of the correspondence theory of truth from ancient times, the "mind as mirror" has played a major role. Gilbert Ryle in *The Concept of Mind* worries about the "mind" and "matter" dualism in post-Cartesian philosophy and attempts to combat what he calls this "Cartesian Myth" of representation. Richard Rorty more recently in his *Philosophy and the Mirror of Nature* revisits this problem, ascribing its source to the "mind as mirror" metaphor, the beginnings of which he traces back to the Greeks. Distinctively, the ocular metaphor as it is framed in the Western dialectic is passive and representational, precluding the social, performative, and perlocutionary dimensions of "knowing" that we have stressed earlier.

In the Western tradition, questions of the distinguishability of mind and matter, of rationality and emotion, are central issues within the philosophy of mind. Neither of these topics is of much interest, however, in classical Chinese thought. On the one hand, the hylozoistic ("matter is animated") notion of *qi* 氣 , the vital energizing field that constitutes all natural processes, renders discussions of the relevance of any psychophysical dualism moot. On the other hand, *xin* 心 (a stylized drawing of the heart), normally translated as "heart-and-mind," precludes the assumption of distinctions between thinking and feeling, or idea and affect. *Xin* is perhaps most frequently translated simply as "heart," but since it is the seat of thinking and judgment, the notion of mind must be included in its characterization if the term is to be properly understood. Indeed, the functional equivalent of what we often think of as "purpose" or "intention" is also to be included in the notion of *xin*.

A first observation is that we have to resist the dualistic understanding of body and its parts as reified corporeality. Taking our cue from Chinese medicine in which the term *zhen mo* 診脈 means "taking a pulse" rather than "examining a blood vessel or artery," we have to think physiologically rather than anatomically. *Xin*, then, is not primarily a thing, but a function, not primarily an anatomical structure, but a physiological process. Bracketing the "What is *xin*?" question as being overly analytic, perhaps we do better to ask the more systemic question: "*How* does *xin* function?"

In the classical period, *xin* is first the function of thinking and feeling, and derivatively, the locus of thinking, an "office" or "occupation" or "organ (*guan* 官)" similar to the other senses. The advantage of *xin* over the other sense occupations, however, is that it is able to think and reflect:

> The organs (*guan* 官) of hearing and of seeing, being unable to reflect, can be misled by external things. When one thing engages another, all it does is draw it to it. But the job of the *xin* is reflecting. When it reflects it gets it, and when it does not, it does not.[29]

The interpenetration of idea, intention, and affect expressed in the notion of *xin* entails the conclusion that thinking is never a dispassionate speculative enterprise, but involves normative judgments which assess the relative merit of the sensations, inclinations, and appetites that constitute our experience of the world and of ourselves. Further, since appetites and ideas are always clothed in some degree with activating "emotion," they are to be understood, more often than not, as *dispositions to act*.

Another implication that follows from the inseparability of feeling and thinking is the practical orientation of most of Chinese thought. If ideas are dispositions to act, what might in other cultural contexts be thought of as theories are little more than wholesale practical recommendations. Thus it is most difficult among the Chinese to find contexts within which the separation of theoretical and practical activities would prevail. When, for example, Confucius says, "From fifteen, my heart-and-mind was set upon learning. . . ,"[30] he is indicating his commitment to a practical regimen aimed at self-realization. Thinking and learning are, within the Chinese tradition, oriented to the practical ends of the moral life. As Mencius observes:

> For a person to realize fully one's heart-and-mind is to realize fully one's nature and character, and in so doing, one realizes nature (*tian* 天).[31]

Going back to Plato, the Western tradition is accustomed to construe efforts aimed at moral perfection as involving an internal struggle between reason and passion, or, with Augustine, between what we know we ought to do, and an obstreperous "will" that frustrates our acting upon that knowledge. In the Chinese world there is little such internal conflict assumed to be involved in ethical development. The unpartitioned self characterized by *xin* means that it is unlikely that we should find Hamlets or St. Pauls prominent among the Chinese.

But then does *xin* even entail a "self" as presumed in Western conceptions of person? Jacques Gernet makes the distinction between the traditional Chinese notions of self and familiar Western concepts by rejecting the relevance of the mind/body and reason/experience disjunctions to the Chinese experience:

> Not only was the substantial opposition between the soul and the body something quite unknown to the Chinese, all souls being, in their view, destined to be dissipated sooner or later, but so was the distinction, originally inseparable from it, between the sensible and the rational. The Chinese had never believed in the existence of a sovereign and independent faculty of reason. The concept of a soul endowed with reason and capable of acting freely for good or for evil, which is so fundamental to Christianity, was alien to them.[32]

If Western notions of "self" are typically framed in terms of the consciousness of an autonomous will or reason, such a self can only refer to one's individuated consciousness in relation to itself. The self, in other words, is self-consciousness. But self-consciousness requires that

47

one is able to objectify one's thoughts, feelings, and so on. Hyper self-consciousness of this sort is a modern Western invention that does not play a role in classical Chinese concerns about personal development.

If in the classical Chinese world the conflict associated with self-realization is not turned inward as a struggle between the heart and the mind—that is, between the passions and reason, between our will and our judgment—what then are the dynamics of personal development? If the dynamic of unrealized selfhood does not entail the self divided against itself, what is the source and the nature of the disturbance that personal discipline is meant to overcome?

It is perhaps in providing a response to such questions that *Tracing Dao to Its Source* makes its most important recommendations. If agitation is not referenced primarily within one's soul, it can only be a disturbance in the relationships which constitute the self in its interactions with external things. Said another way, if a person is not in fact constituted by some essential, partitioned "soul," but is rather seen as a dynamic pattern of personal, social, and natural relationships, agitation must arise as a consequence of poor management of these constitutive roles and relationships. Hence, agitation in the heart-and-mind is not narrowly "psychological," but more properly of broad ethical concern: How should we live and what should we do?

It is *not* through an internal struggle of reason against the passions, but through a mirroring of the things of the world as they are in their relations with us, that we reach a state in which none among the myriad things is able to agitate our hearts and minds, and we are able to promote their flourishing. In other words, we defer to the integrity of those things which contextualize us, thus establishing a frictionless equilibrium with them. And it is this achieved equilibrium that is precisely the relationship most conducive to symbiotic growth and productivity. The Daoist sage in *Zhuangzi* is described in such terms:

> The stillness of the sage is not simply his saying: "Stillness is good!" and hence he is still. Rather, he is still because none of the myriad things is able to disrupt his heart-and-mind. When

water is still, it illuminates one's whiskers and eyebrows, and in its placidity it provides a standard so that the skilled artisan can take his measure from it. If the stillness of water provides illumination, how much more so one's spirits. The stillness of the sage's heart-and-mind is mirror to the whole world and mirror to the myriad things.[33]

Throughout the *Huainanzi* we find reference to this "mirrorlike knowing." For example, in *Huainanzi* 6:

The sage is like a mirror—
He neither sees things off nor goes out to meet them,
He responds to everything without storing anything up.
Thus, he is never injured through the myriad transformations he
   undergoes.

Rules of thumb, customs, standards, methods, stipulated concepts and theories, commandments, principles, laws of natures, conventions— all of these, in requiring us to "welcome things as they come and escort them as they go," result in what Steve Goldberg has described as "a hardening of the categories." Having stored past experience and organized it in the process, we then recall, participate in, and anticipate a world patterned by these discriminations. The sage, however, mirrors the world *at each moment* in a way that is undetermined by the shape of a world passed away, or by anticipations of a world yet to come.

Importantly, the Daoist project is neither passive nor quietistic. Water is a source of nourishment; the mirror is a source of light; the heart-and-mind is a source of transformative energy. To "know" as the mirror "knows" is not representational, but casting the world in a certain light. Such performative "knowing" is to actively interpret and realize a world with healthy, productive effect. These metaphors for *xin* entail presentation rather than representation, and coordination rather than correspondence. "Mirroring" then is best seen as synergistic and responsive, like virtuoso dancing or charioting where all of the elements are in step, and constitute a fluid interdependent whole.

There is, with appropriate Daoist qualification, an "objectively" real world. And the sage does seek to entertain this world as "objectively" as possible. The qualification, then, is that for the Daoist, the objective world is objectless. The world is a flow of events which belies any discriminations that would lay claim to fixity or certainty. "Things" are a gloriously complex yet passing pattern of discriminations that give way to novel patterns in the flux of irrepressible transformation. Hence, when the sage recommends we become "one with all things," it is certainly an exhortation to appreciate the parity and continuities that obtain among them. Perhaps more importantly, however, it is also an encouragement to become one with "this" or "that," reveling in the bottomless particularity and sustained uniqueness of each passing event made possible by the transformation of things (*wuhua* 物化).

> Before long Master Lai fell ill. Wheezing and panting, he was on the brink of death. His wife and children gathered about him and wept. Master Li, having gone to ask after him, scolded them, saying, "Get away! Don't impede his transformations!"
>
> Leaning against the door, Master Li spoke with Master Lai, saying, "Extraordinary, these transformations! What are you going to be made into next? Where are you going to be sent? Will you be made into a rat's liver? Or will you be made into an insect's arm? . . ."[34]

Even terms such as "quiescence" or "stillness (*jing* 靜)" and "emptiness (*xu* 虛)," a vocabulary which in English translation suggests inertia and stasis, are dynamic in this tradition: an achieved balance, a productive harmony, a frictionless equilibrium, steadiness and stability. For example, "emptiness" of the heart-and-mind is receptivity and tolerance. As room to accommodate a boundless amount of experience, it is "emptiness-becoming-full"; as openness to entertain each new experience on its own terms without prejudice, it is "fullness-becoming-empty."

Tracing Dao *to Its Source* takes this active, positive contribution of the unagitated heart-and-mind as a central theme. First, stillness or quiescence is the human being's natural condition:

> A man is quiescent when born—
> This is his Heaven-endowed nature.
> He moves when aroused—
> This is the stirring of that nature.
> The human spirit responds when things come on the scene—
> This is the movement of the intellect. (Section 5)

External things have the power to attract one's attention, arousing one's likes and dislikes, and thus obstructing one's way. This distraction can make a person biased and judgmental, thereby obstructing the natural equilibrium of a situation:

> When the intellect comes into contact with things,
> Feelings of attraction and aversion are produced.
> Where these feelings of attraction and aversion have taken shape,
> And the intellect has been enticed from the outside,
> One is unable to return to himself,
> And the heavenly principles in him are destroyed. (Section 5)

The issue here is the quality of relatedness between the internal and the external. It is not that external things are in themselves pernicious or destructive. Nor is it that the human heart-and-mind is given to producing dissension in the world. In fact, in the vocabulary of classical Chinese thought, the internal (*nei* 內) and the external (*wai* 外) are correlative categories which, like *yin* and *yang*, are properly on an interdependent and mutually entailing continuum, inseparable and indivisible. The goal is to keep the internal and external relations intact (*quan* 全):

> ... [I]nwardly he has that which links him with the trigger of heaven, and so does not give up what he finds in himself for the sake of position, wealth, and ease. (Section 19)

Another way of saying "stillness (*jing* 靜)" that locates this posture relationally between the heart-and-mind and the external world is "nonaction (*wuwei* 無爲)":

> Hence, one who understands *dao*
>> Returns to his limpidity and stillness,
>
> And one who knows all there is to know about things
>> Always ends up with nonactivity. . . .
>
>
>> He succeeds without deliberating,
>> He accomplishes without doing. (Section 10)

How does one lose one's natural equilibrium? By reliance upon small devices that render one "partial" where one should remain "intact (*quan* 全)":

> Thus, those who embody *dao* do not exert themselves yet are
>> never at wits' end
> While those who rely on devices are worn out with nothing to
>> show for it in the end. (Section 7)

The natural posture is "objectless desire (*wu yu* 無欲)" where one accommodates things and transforms together with them without introducing disintegrative factors—likes and dislikes, possession and rejection, approval and disapproval—into the relationship:

> Thus, when a man harbors a calculating heart
>> In his breast,
> The quality of his person is contaminated and his spirituality is
> not kept whole. (Section 7)

Rehearsing the diversity of the myriad things where each finds what is appropriate for its needs, the text rejects "sagely" interventions that upset the productive continuity of nature:

> The myriad things have been so-of-themselves from the
>> beginning—
> What room is there for interference by the sage? (Section 9)

Tracing Dao *to Its Source* rejects those emotions that upset one's equanimity and balance:

> Gladness and anger are a deviation from *dao*; worry and sorrow are a falling from *de*; likes and dislikes are excesses of the heart; cravings and desires are a burden on the nature. (Section 16)

But the rejection of those emotions that entail "partiality" is itself productive of the greatest happiness:

> If a man can get to a state in which there is nothing which he enjoys, there will be nothing he does not enjoy; when there is nothing he does not enjoy, he has then reached the extremity of the highest joy. (Section 16)

As we find repeatedly in this treatise, a more general observation about personal realization is turned to political account:

> . . . [S]agacity lies not in governing others, but rather in getting hold of *dao*; joy lies not in wealth and rank, but rather in gaining the symphonious [*he* 和]. (Section 16)

THE EFFICACY OF ACCOMMODATION

A major theme of *Tracing* Dao *to Its Source* is that accommodation is not passive or weak, but the source of the fullest strength and influence. It is accommodation which is productive of timeliness and efficacy. Where small devices are exclusionary, accommodation is inclusionary, enabling one to extend oneself.

This insight—the efficacy of accommodation—is given specific political application. Liu An's greatest problem was the coercion of the central government and its unwillingness to accommodate the mosaic of local political structures. By invoking the efficacy of the ancient kings, Liu An is recommending the ultimate strength of tolerance and suggesting the counterproductivity of pursuing those political desires that entail coercion.

The efficacy of the "dark *de* (*xuande* 玄德)" is illustrated by the transformative effect that Shun has on his world. Through "genuineness of purpose" and acting through the heart-and-mind, he is able to shape the values and customs of the world to a degree that far exceeds the power of laws and punishments. It is external order effected through inner tranquillity; it is governing the trunk and branches by taking care of the root; it is bringing order to the myriad things by managing the gate from which they emerge.

Bringing the discussion down to the present situation, *Tracing* Dao *to Its Source* addresses the question of how to rule the empire explicitly:

> The empire is something which I possess, while I am also something which the empire possesses. How could there be any gap between the empire and me? Why must "possessing the empire" mean effecting one's edicts and commands by holding authority and power and wielding the handle of life and death? By "possessing the empire" is not meant this, but simply finding it in oneself. If I find it in myself then the empire also finds me in it. If the empire and I find it in each other, then we will always possess each other. Again, how can there be room for anything to be wedged between the empire and me? (Section 19)

The wisdom of this text is that accommodation, inclusivity, tolerance are the real strategies for achieving stable and enduring personal, social, and political order. After all,

> If one knows how to look upon himself as large and the world as small, he is close to *dao*. (Section 16)

ON THE TRANSLATION

We have included the Chinese text along with the translation, and parsed passages to reveal the way in which a concatenation of images is linked by parallel sentence structure, the rhythmic pace of the lines, and the judicious use of rhyme. To illustrate the way in which the text turns from one image or idea to the next, we have introduced section breaks into the English translation that do not occur in the original Chinese. If this is taking an editorial liberty, it should be remembered that the original Chinese text is unpunctuated and unparsed, leaving its readers to discover its rhythm as an integral step in their appreciation of its meaning. We have expended some effort to identify as many of the rhymes as possible, although given the conspiracy of geography, dialect, and the passage of time, any such attempt is necessarily flawed. These rhymes are indicated in the Chinese text with [square brackets].

The Chinese text is adapted from D. C. Lau and Chen Fong Ching (editors), *A Concordance to the Huainanzi*, in the ICS Ancient Chinese Text Concordance Series (Hong Kong: Commercial Press, 1992). The specialist reader is referred to the notes in this source for the resolution of textual problems and suggested emendations.

NOTES TO THE INTRODUCTION

[1] See Michael Loewe (1986).

[2] See Ho Che Wah (1998).

[3] That is, fully a third of *Beginning Reality* is borrowed from our extant 33-chapter *Zhuangzi*, but it was compiled at a time before the imperial librarian Liu Xiang edited the text down from the 52 chapters recorded in the Han dynasty court bibliography. Hence, *Beginning Reality* might well contain parts of the *Zhuangzi* presently lost.

[4] The motivation of "Han thinking," involving as it does the desire to accommodate a variety of often conflicting texts, is certainly not altogether missing from our own tradition. As higher critics have long understood, the Book of Genesis is a literary pastiche sewn together from a variety of authoritative sources. From the perspective of the compilers, each of the narrative strands giving different, often mutually inconsistent, accounts of Creation, owned sufficient authoritativeness that all had to be included as expressions of cultural range and diversity. As such, cultural coherence overrides concerns for logical consistency.

[5] See Robin Yates (1997):10–19 for a summary account of the current discussion on "Huang-Lao."

[6] It is interesting that a thousand years later, during the Tang dynasty, Han Yu would appropriate this same title to make his argument for a new, simplified Confucian orthodoxy purged of the noxious influences of monastic Daoism and Buddhism. A surface reading of Han Yu would make his project the antithesis of the "inclusivity" of Liu An and his colleagues. But in a careful reading of Han Yu's version of *Tracing Dao to Its Source*, we can see that he is a willing appropriator of otherwise competing philosophical ideas. Charles Hartman rehearses Han Yu's argument for the fundamental congruency between classical Confucianism and Mohism, an argument that can be extended to the Daoists and Buddhists as well. See Hartman (1986), especially pp. 145–162.

[7] For an exploration of the meaning of the pervasive water metaphor in the early sources, see Sarah Allan's *The Way of Water and Sprouts of Virtue* (1997).

[8] *Zhuangzi* 5/2/40; cf. translation in Graham (1981):54, and Watson (1968):40 (hereafter G54 and W40, respectively).

[9] *Zhuangzi* 4/2/33 (G54, W40).

[10] For most of the pre-Socratics, *kosmos* was divine, and for both Plato and early Aristotle, *kosmos* was the "visible God" (*horatos theos*).

[11] *Zhuangzi* 63/23/56 (G103, W256).

[12] This phrase is most commonly translated as "standing alone, it does not change." But *gai* 改 is a particular kind of change: It is not transformation (*hua* 化), or change over time (*bian* 變), or substitution (*yi* 易), but rather "improvement" or "correction."

[13] Zhang Dongsun (1995):375.

[14] *Analects* 2/21:

> Someone asked Confucius, "Why do you not take up office in government?" The Master replied, "The *Book of Documents* says: 'Filiality! Simply being filial and being a friend to your brothers extends into exercising governance.' These family virtues are also the stuff of government. Why must one 'take up office in government?'"

[15] *Analects* 2/8:

> Zixia asked about filiality (*xiao*). The Master replied, "The difficulty lies in showing the proper countenance. As for the young contributing their energies when there is work to be done, and deferring to their elders when there is wine and food to be had—how can merely doing this be considered filiality?"

[16] *Analects* 3/12:

> The expression "sacrifice as though present" is taken to mean "sacrifice to the gods as though the gods are present." But the Master said, "If I myself do not participate in the sacrifice, it is as though I have not sacrificed at all."

[17] *Analects* 6/22:

> Fan Chi inquired about wisdom (*zhi*). The Master replied, "To devote yourself to what is appropriate (*yi*) for the people, and to show respect for the gods and spirits while keeping them at a distance can be called wisdom."

See also *Analects* 11/12:

> Zilu asked how to serve the spirits and the gods. The Master replied, "Not yet being able to serve other people, how would you be able to serve the spirits?" He said, "May I ask about death?" The Master replied, "Not yet understanding life, how could you understand death?"

[18] *Xunzi* 63/17/16f.; cf. Knoblock (1994) vol 3:16f.

[19] Graham (1981):85–86.

[20] Zhang (1995):373–374.

[21] *Xunzi* 79/21/22; cf. Knoblock (1994) vol 3:102.

[22] *Zhuangzi* 15/6/9 (G86, W81).

[23] *Zhuangzi* 19/7/2 (G94, W92).

[24] *Zhuangzi* 64/23/72 (G106, W259–260).

[25] See Li Zehou (1987).

[26] *Yijing* 43/*xishang*/9.

[27] To translate this icon as "dragon," as is conventionally done, reflects the difficulties encountered in cultural translation, *long* needing as it does to be

clearly distinguished from its Anglo-Saxon cousin that met a proper end "crushed under the Christian foot of St. George." See John Hay (1994).

[28] Tu Wei-ming (1997):4.

[29] *Mencius* 6A15.

[30] *Analects* 2/5.

[31] *Mencius* 7A1.

[32] Jacques Gernet (1985):147.

[33] *Zhuangzi* 33/13/2 (G259, W142).

[34] *Zhuangzi* 17/6/53 (G88, W85).

PART TWO: TRACING *DAO* TO ITS SOURCE

1 原道訓

夫道者，覆天載地，
廓四方，
柝八極，　　　〔職〕　　[1]
高不可際，
深不可測，　　〔職〕　　[1]
包裹天地，
稟授無形。　　〔耕平〕　[2]
源流泉（滂）〔浡〕，　〔術〕　　[3] [A]
沖而徐盈；　　〔耕平〕　[2]
混混汩汩，　　〔術〕　　[3] [A]
濁而徐清。　　〔耕平〕　[2]

故植之而塞于天地，
橫之而彌于四海，
施之無窮而無所朝夕。　〔鐸〕　　[4] [A]
舒之幎於六合，
卷之不盈於一握。　〔屋〕　　[4] [A]
約〔藥〕而能張，　〔陽平〕　[5]
幽〔幽平〕而能明，　〔陽平〕　[5]
弱〔藥〕而能強，　〔陽平〕　[5]
柔〔幽平〕[1]而能剛。　〔陽平〕　[5]
橫四維而含陰陽，　〔陽平〕　[5]
（絃）〔紘〕宇宙而章三光。　〔陽平〕　[5]
甚淖而𣹰，
甚纖而微。　　〔微平〕　[6] [Tc]

60

Section 1

As for *dao*:

> It shelters the heavens and supports the earth,[1]
> Extends beyond the four points of the compass
> And opens up the eight points of the compass.[2] [1]
> It is high beyond reach
> And deep beyond reckoning; [1]
> It envelops the cosmos,
> And gives to the yet formless. [2]
> Flowing from its source it becomes a gushing spring, [3]
> What was empty slowly becomes full; [2]
> First turbid and then surging forward, [3]
> What was murky slowly becomes clear.[3] [2]

Hence,[4] stand it up vertically, and it stuffs up the heavens and the
earth;

> Lay it horizontally on its side, and it fills the four seas.[5]
> Dealing it out it becomes endless, yet is without morning or
> evening.[6] [4]
> Unroll it, and it blankets the six directions;
> Roll it up, and it is less than a handful. [4]
>> Compact, it can stretch out; [5]
>> Dark, it can be bright; [5]
>> Weak, it can be strong; [5]
>> Pliant, it can be unbending.[7] [5]
>> It stretches over the four cables holding up the
>> heavens, and harbors within itself the *yin* and the
>> *yang*; [5]
>> It broadens the cosmos and brightens the sun, the
>> moon, and the stars. [5]
>> It is the thinnest of gruels,
>> The finest and most subtle texture.[8] [6]

山以之高，
淵以之（深）〔回〕[2]，
獸以之走，
鳥以之飛，　　　〔微平〕　[6] [Tc]
日月以之明，　　〔陽平〕　[7]
星歷以之行，　　〔陽平〕　[7]
麟以之游，
鳳以之翔。　　　〔陽平〕　[7]

泰古二皇，　　　〔陽平〕　[7]
得道之柄，　　　〔陽平〕　[7]
立於中央，　　　〔陽平〕　[7]
神與化游，
以撫四方。　　　〔陽平〕　[7]

是故能天運地滯，　〔祭〕　[8]
輪轉而無廢，　　〔祭〕　[8]
水流而不止，　　〔之上〕　[9]
與萬物終始。　　〔之上〕　[9]
風興雲蒸，　　　〔蒸平〕　[10]
事無不應；　　　〔蒸平〕　[10]
雷聲雨降，　　　〔東平〕　[11]
並應無窮。　　　〔東平〕　[11]
鬼出（電）〔神〕入，　〔緝〕　[12]
龍興鸞集；　　　〔緝〕　[12]
鈞旋轂轉，
周而復匝。　　　〔緝〕　[12]

已彫已琢，　　　〔屋〕　[13]
還反於樸。　　　〔屋〕　[13]

By virtue of it, mountains are high;
By virtue of it, abysses are deep; [6]
By virtue of it, animals run;
By virtue of it, birds fly; [6]
By virtue of it, the sun and moon are bright; [7]
By virtue of it, the stars and celestial bodies rotate; [7]
By virtue of it, the unicorn rambles about;
By virtue of it, the phoenix soars.[9] [7]

Section 2

The two kings, the Tai Huang and the Gu Huang,[10] [7]
Got hold of the handle of *dao* [7]
And stood at the center. [7]
In spirit they roamed together with the demiurge of trans-
    formation
To bring peace to the world. [7]

Hence (working the handles of *dao*), they can:
Move like the heavens and stay still like the earth. [8]
Turning like a wheel without flagging, [8]
Flowing like water without cease, [9]
They begin and end at the same time as the myriad things. [9]
Just as when the wind rises, the clouds steam forth, [10]
There was nothing to which they did not respond; [10]
Just as when the thunder crashes, the rain falls, [11]
They are never at a loss in their response. [11]
Ghosts appear, gods disappear, [12]
Dragons fly away, phoenixes alight. [12]
Like the potter's wheel spinning, like the hub whirling,
Going full circle they start going round again. [12]

Carved and chiseled, [13]
They return to being an uncarved block.[11] [13]

無爲爲之而合于道，無爲言之而通乎德，恬愉無（矜）
〔矜〕而得于和，有萬不同而便于性，神託于秋毫之（未）
〔末〕，而大與宇宙之總。

　　　其德（優）〔覆〕天地而和陰陽，　　〔陽平〕　[14]
　　　　　　節四時而調五行。　　〔陽平〕　[14]
　　　　　　　呴諭覆育，
　　　　　萬物群生[3]，　　〔耕平〕　[14]
　　　　　　潤于草木，
　　　　　　浸于金石，　　〔鐸〕　[15]
　　　　　　禽獸碩大，
　　　　　　毫毛潤澤，　　〔鐸〕　[15]

　　羽翼奮也，角觡生也，獸胎不殰，鳥卵不毈，父無喪子之
憂，兄無哭弟之哀，
　　　　　　童子不孤，
　　　　　　婦人不孀，　　〔陽平〕　[16]
　　　　　　虹蜺不出，　　〔術〕　[17]
　　　　　　賊星不行，　　〔陽平〕　[16]
　　　　　　含德之所致。　　〔質〕　[17]

Doing what they did with no ulterior motive, they accorded with *dao*; saying what they said with no ulterior motive, they were in communion with *de*; happy and easy with no sense of self-importance, what they gained was in harmony; though they had a myriad of different manifestations,[12] they yet accorded with each of these things in their various natures; their spirits resided in the tiniest tip of an autumn down, and yet were larger than the sum total of the cosmos.

> Their *de* embraced the heavens and the earth and brought
> harmony to the *yin* and the *yang*, [14]
> Ordered the four seasons and regulated the five phases. [14]
>> Brooding over things and nurturing them,
>> They produced the myriad things in all their
>> variety.[13] [14]
>> They provided moistening nourishment to the
>> grasses and trees
>> And penetrated the minerals and rocks. [15]
>> The birds and beasts grew large and tall
>> With coats glossy and sleek, [15]
> Wings sprouting out and horns growing,[14] animals did not miscarry and birds did not lay addled eggs, fathers were spared the suffering of mourning their sons and elder brothers were spared the grief of weeping over the younger ones,
>> Children were not orphaned
>> Nor were wives widowed, [16]
>> Evil confluences of the *yin* and the *yang* did not
>> appear [17]
>> Nor did ominous celestial portents occur.[15] [16]
> This all came of the *de* they harbored within. [17]

夫太上之道，

生萬物而不有，　　〔之上〕　[18]
成化像而弗宰。　　〔之上〕　[18]

跂行喙息，蠉飛蝡動，待而後生，莫之知德；待之後死，莫之能怨。得以利者不能譽，用而敗者不能非。

收聚畜積而不加富，
布施稟授而不益貧。　〔諄平〕　[19]
旋（縣）〔絲〕而不可究，
纖微而不可勤。　　〔諄平〕　[19]
累之而不高，
墮之而不下，　　　〔魚上〕　[20]
益之而不眾，
損之而不寡，　　　〔魚上〕　[20]
斲之而不薄，
殺之而不殘，　　　〔元平〕　[21]
鑿之而不深，
填之而不淺。　　　〔元平〕　[21]
忽兮怳兮，　　　　〔陽上〕　[22]
不可爲象兮；　　　〔陽上〕　[22]
怳兮忽兮，　　　　〔術〕　　[23]
用不屈兮；　　　　〔術〕　　[23]
幽兮冥兮，　　　　〔耕平〕　[24]

66

The primordial *dao*:

> Engenders the myriad things without appropriating
> them, [18]
> Molds things into various shapes by the process of transfor-
> mation without claiming stewardship over them.[16] [18]

Creatures moving about on legs and breathing through their
mouths, insects wriggling and flying about—they owe their life to it,
yet realize not they ought to be grateful; they owe their death to it, yet
are incapable of harboring a grudge.[17] Those who benefit from it
cannot sing its praises, while those who fail through it cannot con-
demn it.

> Regardless of how much is gathered and stored it is none the
> richer;
> Regardless of how much is doled out and bestowed it is none
> the poorer. [19]
> So minute and tenuous—yet there is no getting to the bot-
> tom of it;
> So fine and subtle—yet there is no using it up. [19]
> Piling it up does not make it taller,
> Collapsing it does not make it shorter; [20]
> Adding to it does not make it more numerous,
> Taking away from it does not make it less numerous; [20]
> Whittling it away does not make it thinner,
> Slaughtering does not leave it devastated; [21]
> Boring into it does not make it deeper,
> Filling it in does not make it shallower. [21]
> > Hazy and nebulous, [22]
> > It cannot be taken as an image; [22]
> > Nebulous and hazy, [23]
> > It is not spent through use; [23]
> > Obscure and dark, [24]

應無形兮；　　〔耕平〕　[24]

遂兮洞兮，　　〔東上〕　[25]

不虛動兮。　　〔東上〕　[25]

與剛柔卷舒兮，

與陰陽俛仰兮。

昔者馮夷、大丙之御也，　〔魚去〕　[26] [A]

乘（雲）〔雷〕車，

（入）〔六〕雲蜺，　　〔支平〕　[27] [A]

游微霧，　　　〔魚去〕　[26] [A]

騖（悗忽）〔忽悗〕，　〔陽上〕　[28]

歷遠彌高以極往，　　　〔陽上〕　[28]

經霜雪而無迹，　　　　〔錫〕　[27] [A]

照日光而無景，　　　　〔陽上〕　[28]

扶搖抮抱羊角而上，　　〔陽上〕　[28]

經紀山川，　　〔諄平〕　[29]

蹈騰崑崙，　　〔諄平〕　[29]

排閶闔，

淪天門。　　〔諄平〕　[29]

末世之御，　　〔魚去〕　[30] [A]

雖有輕車良馬，　〔魚上〕　[30] [A]

勁策利（鍛）〔鍜〕，

不能與之爭先。　〔諄平〕　[29]

是故大丈夫恬然無思，

澹然無慮；　　〔魚平〕　[31]

以天爲蓋，

以地爲輿；　　〔魚平〕　[31]

68

It responds to what is without form; [24]

Deep and dark, [25]

It makes no move in vain.[18] [25]

It is rolled up and unrolled along with the pliant and the
unbending;

It turns upwards and downwards with the *yin* and the *yang*.

Section 4

In their charioting, Ping Yi and Da Bing of antiquity:[19] [26]

Mounted the thunder chariot

And used the cloud dragons as their six horses. [27]

They rambled about in the fine mists, [26]

Galloped around in the hazy and nebulous, [28]

And, ever more distant and ever higher, they made the trip
of all trips. [28]

They would pass over frost and snow without
leaving tracks,[20] [27]

And with the sun shining on them they would cast
no shadow. [28]

Swirling on a typhoon they spiraled upward,[21] [28]

Negotiating mountains and rivers [29]

And leaping over the peaks of Kunlun,[22] [29]

They pushed open the Changhe gates[23]

And entered through the Gateway of Heaven.[24] [29]

A charioteer in an age in decline: [30]

Even with a light vehicle, fine horses, [30]

A strong whip and sharp goads,

Cannot hope to overtake them. [29]

Hence, the person of great stature:[25]

Being placidly free of all worries

And serenely without thoughts for the morrow, [31]

Has the heavens as his canopy,

The earth as his boxframe, [31]

69

四時爲馬，

陰陽爲（御）〔驂〕[4]；　　〔魚平〕　[32]

乘雲陵霄，

與造化者俱。　　〔魚平〕　[32]

縱志舒節，

以馳大區。　　〔魚平〕　[32]

可以步而步，　　〔魚去〕　[33] [A]

可以驟而驟。　　〔魚去〕　[33] [A]

（今）〔令〕雨師灑道，

使風伯掃塵。　　〔諄平〕　[34]

電以爲鞭策，

雷以爲車輪。　　〔諄平〕　[34]

上游于霄霓之野，

下出于無垠〔鄂〕之門。　　〔諄平〕　[34]

劉覽（偏）〔徧〕照，

復守以全。　　〔元平〕　[34]

經營四隅，　　〔魚平〕　[35]

還反於樞[5]。　　〔魚平〕　[35]

故以天爲蓋，則無不覆也；　　〔職〕　[36]

以地爲輿，則无不載也；　　〔之去〕　[36]

四時爲馬，則無不使也；　　〔之去〕　[37]

陰陽爲（御）〔驂〕，則無不備也。　　〔之去〕　[37]

是故疾而不搖，　　〔宵平〕　[38]

遠而不勞，　　〔宵平〕　[38]

四支不（動）〔勤〕，　　〔諄平〕　[39]

聰明不損，　　〔諄上〕　[39]

The four seasons as his horses,

And the *yin* and the *yang* as his charioteer.[32]

He mounts the clouds and climbs beyond the skies,

To be with the demiurge of change. [32]

Doing as he pleases and following a freer rhythm

He gallops the great abode. [32]

He walks his horses when he should walk them, [33]

He runs them hard when he should run them. [33]

He gets the god of rain to sprinkle his path

And the god of wind to sweep away the dust.[26] [34]

With lightning as his whip

And thunder as his wheels, [34]

Above he rambles in the free and roaming vastness,

Below he goes out of the gates of boundlessness. [34]

Having scanned all round and left nothing out,

Remaining whole he returns to guard what is within. [34]

He manages the four corners of the earth [35]

Yet always returns to the pivot. [35]

Thus, with the heavens as his canopy, there is nothing that
is unsheltered; [36]

With the earth as his boxframe, there is nothing that has no
conveyance; [36]

With the four seasons as horses, there is nothing that is
unemployed; [37]

With the *yin* and the *yang* as charioteers, there is nothing that
is lacking. [37]

Hence, he travels fast without pitching [38]

And travels far without fatigue. [38]

Without taxing his four limbs [39]

And without draining the keenness of his hearing and
sight, [39]

而知八紘九野之形埒者，何也？執道（要）之柄，而游於無窮
之地〔也〕。

是故天下之事，不可爲也，
　　　　因其自然而推之。　　　〔微平〕　[40] [Ta]
萬物之變，不可究也，
秉其要〔趣而〕歸之（趣）。　　〔微平〕　[40] [Ta]

夫鏡水之與形接也，不設智故而方圓曲直弗能逃也。是故
響不肆應，而景不一設，（叫）〔叫〕呼仿佛，默然自得。

　　　　　　　人生而靜，　　〔耕去〕　[41] [A]
　　　　　　　天之性也。　　〔耕去〕　[41] [A]
　　　　　　　感而後動，　　〔東上〕　[42] [A]
　　性之（害）〔容〕[6]也。　〔東上〕　[42] [A]
　　　　　　　物至而神應，
　　　　　　　知之動也。　　〔東上〕　[42] [A]
　　　　　　　知與物接，
　　　　　　　而好憎生焉。　〔耕平〕　[43] [A]
　　　　　　　好憎成形，　　〔耕平〕　[43] [A]
　　　　　　　而知誘於外，　〔祭〕　　[44] [A]
　　　　　　　不能反己，
　　　　　　　而天理滅矣。　〔月〕　　[44] [A]

72

He knows the lay and the boundaries of the various divisions and quadrants of the cosmos. How is this so? It is because he has his hands on the control handles of *dao* and rambles in the land of the inexhaustible.

Hence, there is nothing you can do about the world.

> You can only follow what is natural in pushing the myriad
> things ahead. [40]
> There is no getting to the bottom of the changes they
> undergo.
> You can only grasp the essential destination and lead them
> there. [40]

Section 5

It is because the mirror and water do not, in anticipation, equip themselves with cleverness, that the shapes they come into contact with cannot but show themselves as they are: square, round, bent, and straight.[27] Hence, an echo does not resound as it likes, and a shadow is not something that is cast once and for all. The likeness of the sound and shape is attained without fuss.

> A man is quiescent when born— [41]
> This is his Heaven-endowed nature. [41]
> He moves when aroused— [42]
> This is the stirring of that nature. [42]
> The human spirit responds when things come on the scene—
> This is the movement of the intellect. [42]
> When the intellect comes into contact with things,
> Feelings of attraction and aversion are produced. [43]
> Where these feelings of attraction and aversion have taken
> shape, [43]
> And the intellect has been enticed from the outside, [44]
> One is unable to return to himself,
> And the Heavenly principles in him are destroyed. [44]

故達於道者，

不以人易天，　　〔眞平〕　[45]

外與物化，

而內不失其情。　〔耕平〕　[45]

至無而供其求，

時騁而要其宿。

小大脩短，

各有其具，　　〔魚去〕　[46]

萬物之至，

騰踴肴亂

而不失其數。　　〔魚去〕　[46]

是以處上而民弗重〔也〕，

居前而眾弗害〔也〕，

天下歸之，　　〔微平〕　[47]

姦邪畏之。　　〔微平〕　[47]

以其無爭於萬物也，故莫（敢）〔能〕與之爭。

夫臨江而釣，曠日而不能盈羅，雖有鉤箴芒距，微綸芳
餌，加之以詹何、娟嬛之數，猶不能與網罟爭得也。射者
（扞）〔扜〕烏號之弓，彎綦衛之箭，

74

Thus, one who understands *dao*

> Does not barter what belongs to Heaven for what is
> man's.[28] [45]
> While externally he is transformed along with the trans-
> formation of things,
> Internally he does not become other than what he is really
> like. [45]
> Lacking in everything, he is able to satisfy their needs.
> Though constantly on the move, he will always be waiting for
> them where they put up for the night.
>> Everything regardless of size or shape
>> Is equipped with what it properly ought to have.[29] [46]
>> Though the myriad things come bounding along
>> In utter disarray,
>> He does not lose his count on them. [46]

Therefore, he is on top of the people, yet they do not find him heavy;
> He is in front of the multitude, yet they do not find he blocks
> the view.
>> The empire turns to him [47]
>> And the evil and depraved fear him. [47]
It is because he does not contend with the myriad things that none
are able to contend with him.[30]

Section 6

A person can fail to fill his basket after spending an entire day
fishing beside the river. Though he has all manner of hooks, barbs,
and lures, uses fine line and tempting bait, and in addition to this,
has the technique of a Zhan He or Juan Xuan,[31] he won't be able to
vie with the fishing nets in the size of the catch. Though an archer in
shooting birds in flight draws the Wu Hao bow,[32] fits a fine arrow of
Qi to the bowstring,

重之〔以〕羿、逢蒙子之巧，　　〔幽上〕　[48] [A]

以要飛鳥，　　〔幽上〕　[48] [A]

猶不能與羅者競多。何則？以所持之小也。張天下以爲之籠，因江海以爲〔之〕（罟）〔罛〕，又何亡魚失鳥之有乎？

故（夫）〔矢〕不若繳，

繳不若〔網〕，　　〔陽上〕　[49]

〔網不若〕無形之像。　〔陽上〕　[49]

夫釋大道而任小數，　　〔魚上〕　[50] [A]

無以異於使蟹（蛑）〔捕〕鼠，　〔魚上〕　[50] [A]

蟾蠩捕蚤，　　〔幽上〕　[50] [A]

不足以禁姦塞邪，亂乃逾滋。

昔者夏鯀作（三）〔九〕仞之城，諸侯背之，海外有狡心。禹知天下之叛也，乃壞城平池，散財物，焚甲兵，

施之以德，　　〔職〕　　[51]

海外賓服，　　〔職〕　　[51]

四夷納職，　　〔職〕　　[51]

合諸侯於塗山，

執玉帛者萬國。　〔職〕　　[51]

故機械之心　　〔侵平〕　[52] [A]

藏於胸中，　　〔東平〕　[52] [A]

And reinforces this with the expertise of an Yi or Feng
    Mengzi,[33] [48]
He still won't be able to vie with the nets in the number of
    birds he catches. [48]
Why is this so? It is because what he has in hand is small. If one
stretches the world as his bird-basket and converts the rivers and seas
into a fishnet, how will a fish or a bird ever manage to get away![34]
Thus, an arrow is not as effective as a corded arrow,

    A corded arrow is not as effective as a net, [49]
    And a net is not as effective as the Formless Image.[35] [49]
    To let go of the great *dao* and rely on small devices [50]
    Is no different from trying to use a crab to catch a mouse [50]
    Or a toad to catch a flea— [50]
Far from these devices being adequate to prohibit wickedness and
stem depravity, disorder will in fact be on the increase.

Section 7

In ancient times, Gun of Xia[36] constructed city walls eighty feet
high, yet the various nobles turned against him and in the lands
beyond the seas men became crafty. (His son) Yu, realizing that the
world was disaffected, demolished the walls, filled in the moats, gave
away the accumulated wealth, burned the armor and weapons,

    And treated all with beneficence. [51]
    The lands beyond the seas acknowledged his suzerainty [51]
    And the barbarian tribes came to offer their tributes. [51]
    And when he assembled the various nobles at Tushan,
    There were ten thousand states bringing gifts of ceremonial
        jade and cloth.[37] [51]

Thus, when a man harbors a calculating heart [52]
    In his breast, [52]

則純白不粹，神德不全，在身者不知，何遠之所能懷！是故革堅則兵利，城成則衝生，若以湯沃沸，亂乃逾甚。

是故鞭噬狗，	〔魚上〕	[53]	[A]
策（虢）〔踶〕馬，	〔魚上〕	[53]	[A]
而欲教之，			
雖伊尹、造父弗能化。	〔歌去〕	[53]	[A]
欲寅之心，	〔侵平〕	[54]	[A]
亡於中，	〔東平〕	[54]	[A]
則飢虎可尾，	〔脂上〕	[55]	[A]
何況狗馬之類乎！	〔微去〕	[55]	[A]
故體道者逸而不窮，	〔東平〕	[56]	
任數者勞而無功。	〔東平〕	[56]	

夫峭法刻誅者，非霸王之業也；箠策繁用者，非致遠之（術）〔御〕也。離朱之明，察箴末於百步之外，〔而〕不能見淵中之魚。師曠之聰，合八風之調，而不能聽十里之外。故任一人之能，

不足以治三畝之宅也。	〔鐸〕	[57]	[A]

The quality of his person is contaminated and his spirituality is not kept whole.[38] If a man lacks knowledge of what is harbored in his own person, how is he going to be able to win over those at a distance? Hence, stronger armor calls forth sharper weapons; the erection of city walls calls forth the battering ram for breaching them.[39] It is like using boiling water to calm water on the boil—the agitation will grow even worse.

Hence, this can be likened to whipping a mad dog [53]
    Or taking a crop to a kicking horse, [53]
    With the intention of training them.
    Even a Yi Yin or a Zao Fu would be unable to transform
        them.[40] [53]
    But where one does not harbor [54]
    A heart that covets its meat, [54]
    He can pull the tail of even a hungry tiger. [55]
    How much more the tails of animals such as horses and
        dogs! [55]
    Thus, those who embody *dao* do not exert themselves yet are
        never at wits' end [56]
    While those who rely on devices are worn out with nothing
        to show for it in the end. [56]

Section 8

Harsh laws and severe punishments are not practices that will perpetuate hegemony or kingship, and the repeated use of a horse-whip is not the way to get to a distant destination. With eyesight that enables him to make out the point of a needle beyond a hundred paces, Li Zhu was not able to spot fishes in the deep.[41] With hearing that enables him to bring the sound of the eight winds into a harmony,[42] Music Master Kuang was not able to hear beyond ten *li*.[43] Thus, if we rely on the ability of one man:

    The management of even a half-acre tract of land will be too
        much for us, [57]

（脩）〔循〕道理之數，　〔魚去〕　[57] [A]

因天地之自然，　〔元平〕　[58] [A]

則六合不足均也。　〔眞平〕　[58] [A]

是故禹之決瀆也，　〔屋〕　[59] [A]

因水以爲師；

神農之播穀也，　〔屋〕　[59] [A]

因苗以爲教。

夫（萍）〔蘋〕樹根於水，

木樹根於土，　〔魚上〕　[60]

鳥排虛而飛，

獸蹠實而走，　〔魚上〕　[60]

蛟龍水居，

虎豹山處，　〔魚上〕　[60]

天地之性也。

兩木相摩而然，

金火相守而流，　〔幽平〕　[61]

員者常轉，

竅者主浮，　〔幽平〕　[61]

自然之勢也。

是故春風至則甘雨降，生育萬物，

羽者嫗伏，　〔職〕　[62] [A]

毛者孕育，　〔沃〕　[62] [A]

草木榮華，

鳥獸卵胎，

莫見其爲者，　〔歌平〕　[63] [A]

而功既成矣。　〔耕平〕　[64] [A]

秋風下霜，　〔陽平〕　[65]

到生挫傷，　〔陽平〕　[65]

80

But if we leave *dao* to its own devices [57]

    And base ourselves on the natural course of the cosmos, [58]

    Then the regulation of all of the universe—up, down, and in
        all directions—is not worth bothering about. [58]

Hence, Yu in draining the accumulated waters [59]

    Took the water as his mentor,

    And Shen Nong in sowing grain [59]

    Took seedlings as model for his instruction.[44]

Section 9

Floating plants take root in water,

    Land plants take root in the soil, [60]

    Birds fly by stroking emptiness,

    Animals run by treading solidity. [60]

    Alligators and dragons make their home in water,

    Tigers and leopards dwell in the mountains. [60]

    This is the nature of the world.

    Two pieces of wood when rubbed together ignite;

    When kept close to fire, metal becomes molten;[45] [61]

    Round things normally spin,

    Hollow things chiefly float. [61]

    It is their natural inclination to do so.

Hence, when the spring winds come they bring the timely rains, and
    the myriad things are produced and nourished.[46]

    Feathered creatures incubate and hatch their eggs, [62]

    Furred creatures conceive and give birth to their young, [62]

    Plants and trees bloom

    And birds and animals are oviparous and viviparous.[47]

    Without anyone ever seeing the actual doing, [63]

    The deed is accomplished. [64]

    When the autumn winds bring the frost, [65]

    Vegetation is injured and snaps, [65]

鷹鷂搏鷙，

昆蟲蟄藏，　　〔陽平〕　[65]

草木注根，　　〔諄平〕　[66] [A]

魚繁湊淵，　　〔眞平〕　[66] [A]

莫見其爲者，　〔歌平〕　[63] [A]

滅而無形[7]〔矣〕。　〔耕平〕　[64] [A]

木處榛巢，

水居窟穴，　　〔質〕　　[67]

禽獸有（芃）〔芃〕，

人民有室，　　〔質〕　　[67]

陸處宜牛馬，

舟行宜多水，　〔微上〕　[68]

匈奴出穢裘，

干、越生葛絺[8]，〔微上〕　[68]

各生所急　　　〔絹〕　　[69]

以備燥溼，　　〔絹〕　　[69]

各因所處　　　〔魚上〕　[70]

以御寒暑，　　〔魚上〕　[70]

並得其宜，

物便其所。　　〔魚上〕　[70]

由此觀之，　　〔元平〕　[71]

萬物固以自然，〔元平〕　[71]

聖人又何事焉！〔元平〕　[71]

九疑之南，　　〔侵平〕　[72]

陸事寡而水事眾，〔東平〕　[72]

於是民人　　　〔眞平〕　[73]

Eagles and falcons sweep down on their prey,
Swarming insects hibernate, [65]
Plants and trees put down their roots, [66]
And fishes and turtles make for the deep. [66]
Without anyone ever seeing the actual doing, [63]
Things disappear without a trace. [64]

Tree dwellers nest in the foliage,
Water dwellers live in underwater caves. [67]
Birds and beasts have beds of straw,
Human beings have houses. [67]
For dwelling on land the rearing of cattle and horses is
    suitable,
And for travel by boat abundance in waterways is
    suitable. [68]
The Xiongnu territory produces animal hides for clothing,
While the Wu and Yue territories produce hemp for
    garments. [68]
Each produces what is badly needed [69]
In defense against the dry and wet; [69]
Each takes advantage of the places in which they are
    situated [70]
To ward off the cold and heat. [70]
They all get what is suitable,
And what is produced meets a local need. [70]
Viewing it from this perspective, [71]
The myriad things have been so-of-themselves from the
    beginning— [71]
What room is there for interference by the sage? [71]
To the south of the Jiuyi mountain region, [72]
There is little to be done on land whereas there is much to be
    done in the water. [72]
For this reason, the people [73]

（被）〔劗〕髮文身， 〔眞平〕 [73]

以像鱗蟲， 〔東平〕 [72]

短綣不袴，

以便涉游， 〔幽平〕 [74]

短袂攘卷，

以便刺舟， 〔幽平〕 [74]

因之也。 〔眞平〕 [75] [A]

鴈門之北， 〔職〕 [76]

狄不穀食， 〔職〕 [76]

賤長貴壯，

俗上氣力， 〔職〕 [76]

人不弛弓，

馬不解勒， 〔職〕 [76]

便之也。 〔元平〕 [75] [A]

故禹之（裸）〔倮〕國，

解衣而入，

衣帶而出，

因之也。 〔眞平〕 [75] [A]

今夫徙樹者，失其陰陽之性，則莫不枯槁。故橘、樹之江
北則化而爲（枳）〔橙〕，

鴝（鵒）〔鵒〕不過濟， 〔脂上〕 [77] [A]

貉度汶而死， 〔脂上〕 [77] [A]

形性不可易，勢居不可移也。

Cut their hair and tattoo their bodies [73]
To look like scaly reptiles. [72]
They wear briefs in place of trousers
For wading and swimming; [74]
They have their short sleeves rolled up
For poling their boats. [74]
This is to avail themselves of what is convenient for the
    environment. [75]
To the north of the Yanmen Pass, [76]
The Di barbarians do not eat grain. [76]
They set great store by men in their prime and look down on
    the aged,
And it is custom to value virility. [76]
Men never slacken their bowstrings
Nor do they unbridle their horses, [76]
In order to be ever on the ready. [75]
Thus, when Yu went to the Country of the Naked,
He took off his clothing before entering
And put it on again before departing.
This was basing his actions on local custom.[48] [75]

Section 10

If in transplanting trees a person neglects the natural balance of
their *yin* and *yang*, they will all wither up and die. Thus: when the
tangerine tree is carried north across the Yangtze River, it is transformed into the bitter-orange tree.

The gray thrush does not cross the Ji River, [77]
And the badger dies when it crosses the Wen River.[49] [77]
Their form and basic nature should not be changed, and neither
should the circumstances under which they live be altered.

是故達於道者，
　　　　反於清靜；　　〔耕去〕　　[78] [A]
　　　究於物者，
　　　終於無爲。
　　　以恬養性，　　　〔耕去〕　　[78] [A]
　　　以漠處神，　　　〔眞平〕　　[79]
　　　則入于天門。　　〔諄平〕　　[79]

　　　所謂天者，　　　〔眞平〕　　[80] [A]
　　　純粹樸素，　　　〔魚去〕　　[81]
　　　質直皓白，　　　〔鐸〕　　　[81]
未始有與雜糅者也。　　〔幽平〕　　[82] [A]
　　　所謂人者，　　　〔眞平〕　　[80] [A]
　　　偶瞇智故，　　　〔魚去〕　　[83]
　　　曲巧僞詐，　　　〔魚去〕　　[83]
所以俛仰於世人
而與俗交者〔也〕。　　〔宵平〕　　[82] [A]

故牛歧蹏而戴角，　　〔屋〕　　　[84] [A]
馬被髦而全足者，　　〔屋〕　　　[84] [A]
　　　天也。　　　　〔眞平〕　　[85] [A]
　　　絡馬之口，
　　　穿牛之鼻者，
　　　人也。　　　　〔眞平〕　　[85] [A]
循天〔眞平〕[9] 者，與道游者也。　　〔幽平〕　　[86] [A]
隨人〔眞平〕者，與俗交者也。　　〔宵平〕　　[86] [A]

86

Hence, one who understands *dao*

    Returns to his limpidity and stillness, [78]

    And one who knows all there is to know about things

    Always ends up with nonactivity.

    If one nourishes his nature with tranquillity [78]

    And lodges his spirit in emptiness,[50] [79]

    Then he has entered the Gateway of Heaven. [79]

By "Heaven" is meant [80]

    Pure and unadulterated like uncarved wood and undyed
        silk, [80]

    Original simplicity and sheer whiteness, [81]

    Which has never been admixed with anything else. [81]

By "man" is meant [80]

    Studying each other and exercising one's knowledge and
        presuppositions, [83]

    Being crafty and deceptive to others, [83]

    In order to get on in the world

    And to be able to deal with the vulgar. [82]

Thus, an ox's having cloven hoofs and horns, [84]

    And a horse's having a mane and uncloven hoofs [84]

        Is what is "Heaven"; [85]

    Bridling a horse's mouth

    And boring an ox's nose

        Is "man."[51] [85]

    Those who follow Heaven ramble about with *dao*, [86]

    Whereas those who accede to man have dealings with the
        vulgar. [86]

夫井魚不可與語大，拘於隘也；夏蟲不可與語寒，篤於時也；

曲士不可與語至道[10]，　　〔幽去〕　[87] [A]
拘於俗，束於教也。　　〔宵去〕　[87] [A]

故聖人不以人滑天，　　〔眞平〕　[88]
不以欲亂情，　　〔耕平〕　[88]
不謀而當，
不言而信，　　〔眞平〕　[88]
不慮而得，
不爲而成，　　〔耕平〕　[88]
精通于靈府，
與造化者爲人。　　〔眞平〕　[88]

夫善游者溺，
善騎者墮，　　〔歌上〕　[89]
各以其所好，
反自爲禍。　　〔歌上〕　[89]
是故好事者未嘗不中，　　〔東平〕　[90]
爭利者未嘗不窮也。　　〔東平〕　[90]

昔共工之力，觸不周之山，
使地東南傾。　　〔耕平〕　[91] [A]
與高辛爭爲帝，
遂潛于淵，　　〔眞平〕　[91] [A]
宗族殘滅，　　〔質〕　[92] [A]

Now, the reason that one cannot discuss the "big" with fish in a well is because they are cooped up in a narrow space. The reason that one cannot discuss "winter" with summer insects is because their life is restricted to one season.

> The reason that we cannot discuss "the ultimate *dao*" with
> > someone whose knowledge is partial [87]
> Is because he is bound by vulgar customs and fettered by
> > what he has been taught.[52] [87]

Thus, the sage does not adulterate Heaven with man, [88]
> And does not allow desire to disturb his actual nature. [88]
> He hits the mark without planning,
> His word is trusted without his having to speak, [88]
> He succeeds without deliberating,
> He accomplishes without doing.[53] [88]
> His purity reaches up to the mansion of the spirits
> And he is a comrade of the demiurge of change. [88]

Section 11

> A good swimmer is sure to drown,
> And a good rider is sure to fall from his mount. [89]
> Each through what he is fond of doing
> Ironically brings calamity on himself. [89]
> Hence, one who is fond of meddling is never known to
> > escape injury, [90]
> And one who contends over profit always ends up in
> > desperate straits. [90]

In ancient times, Gong Gong butted the Buzhou mountain so
> violently
> > That it caused the earth to slope to the southeast, [91]
> > But in contending with Gao Xin for the throne,
> > He ended up in a watery grave, [91]
> > With his clan exterminated, [92]

〔維〕〔繼〕嗣絕祀。　〔之上〕　[93] [A]

越王翳逃山穴，　〔質〕　[92] [A]

越人熏而出之，　〔術〕　[92] [A]

遂不得已。　〔之上〕　[93] [A]

由此觀之，

得在時，不在爭；　〔耕去〕　[94]

治在道，不在聖。　〔耕去〕　[94]

土處下，不爭高，

故安而不危；　〔歌平〕　[95] [A]

水下流，不爭先，

故疾而不遲[11]。　〔脂平〕　[95] [A]

昔舜耕於歷山，朞年，而田者爭處境埒，以封（壤）〔畔〕肥饒相讓；釣於河濱，朞年，而漁者爭處湍瀨，以曲隈深潭相予。當此之時，口不設言，手不指麾，

執玄德於心，

而化馳若神。　〔眞平〕　[96] [A]

使舜無其志，

雖口辯而戶說之，　〔之平〕　[97] [A]

不能化一人。　〔眞平〕　[96] [A]

是故不道之道，

莽乎大哉[12]！　〔之平〕　[97] [A]

And his ancestral sacrifices coming to an end.[54] [93]

King Yi of Yue, on the other hand, fled to the mountain
    caves, [92]

But the people of Yue smoked him out [92]

And ultimately he had no choice but to become their
    king.[55] [93]

Viewing it from this perspective:

Success lies in the opportune moment and not in
    contention;[56] [94]

Orderly government lies in *dao* and not in the sagacious
    leader. [94]

Because earth dwells below and does not contend for a higher
    station,

It is safe and secure; [95]

Because water flows downward and does not contend for the
    lead,

It flows rapidly instead of slowly. [95]

In antiquity, Shun tilled land in the Li mountain area, and in a year, the farmers were vying to occupy the stony and barren land, yielding the rich and fertile plots to others; when he fished on the banks of the river, in a year, the fishermen were contending to occupy the stretches of shallow, rushing water, yielding the nooks and deep pools to others. At that time, he spoke no words of instruction nor gestured any commands,

And yet, because he harbored dark *de*[57] in his heart,

His transforming influence galloped everywhere with spirited
    efficacy. [96]

Had Shun not been genuine in his purpose,

Even if he were to try to win them over by persuasion from
    door to door, [97]

He would still be unable to transform even a single person. [96]

Hence, great indeed is the unspoken *dao*![58] [97]

夫能理三苗，

　　　　朝羽民，　　　〔眞平〕　　[98] [A]

（從）〔徙〕裸國，

　　　　納肅愼[13]，　　　〔眞平〕　　[98] [A]

　未發號施令而移風易俗者，其唯心行者乎！法度刑罰，何足以致之也？是故聖人內修其本，而不外飾其末，保其精神，偃其智故，漠然無爲而無不爲也，澹然無治（也）而無不治也。所謂無爲者，不先物爲也；所謂〔無〕不爲者，因物之所爲〔也〕。所謂無治者，不易自然也；所謂無不治者，因物之相然也。

　　　　萬物有所生，

　　　而獨知守其根；　　〔諄平〕　　[99]

　　　　百事有所出，

　　　而獨知守其門。　　〔諄平〕　　[99]

　故窮無窮，極無極，照物而不眩，響應而不乏，此之謂天解。

To be able to govern the San Miao,

> Bring the Yu people to court, [98]
> Draw the Country of the Naked
> And the Su Shen into the Chinese orbit, [98]

And to be able to transform customs and conventions without issuing orders or commands, is to act secretly within one's heart.[59] How could legal restrictions and punishments in themselves ever be enough to bring this about! Hence, the sage inwardly cultivates that which is the root instead of outwardly putting ornament on that which is the tip. He preserves his spirit and puts aside his cleverness. Quiescently he does nothing, yet leaves nothing undone; serenely he does not impose order on anything, yet there is nothing that is not ordered. By "doing nothing" is meant not being ahead of things in taking action; by "leaving nothing undone" is meant making use of what is done by other things; by "not imposing order" is meant not putting in a substitute for what is so-of-itself; by "nothing not being properly ordered" is meant making use of the mutual recognition that obtains among things.

Section 12

> The myriad things have their progenitor,
> Yet he alone knows to abide by the root; [99]
> The events of the world have a source out of which
> they come,
> Yet he alone knows to abide by the gateway.[60] [99]

Thus, to get to the end of that which has no end and to get to the bounds of that which has no bounds, to go on throwing back the image of things without getting dizzy and to go on responding to sounds without running out of echoes: this is what is called "Heaven's release."

故得道者志弱而事强，　　〔陽平〕　[100]

心虛而應當。　　〔陽平〕　[100]

所謂志弱者，

柔毳安靜，

藏於不敢，

行於不能，　　〔之平〕　[101]

恬然無慮，

動不先時，　　〔之平〕　[101]

與萬物回周旋轉，

不爲先唱，

感而應之。　　〔之平〕　[101]

是故貴者必以賤爲號，

而高者必以下爲基。　　〔之平〕　[101]

託小以包大，　　〔祭〕　[102]

在中以制外，　　〔祭〕　[102]

行柔而剛，　　〔陽平〕　[103]

用弱而强，　　〔陽平〕　[103]

轉化推移，　　〔歌平〕　[104]

得一之道，

而以少正多。　　〔歌平〕　[104]

所謂（其）事强者，

遭變應卒[14]，　　〔元去〕　[105] [Tb]

排患[15] 扞難，　　〔元去〕　[105] [Tb]

力無不勝，　　〔蒸平〕　[106]

敵無不淩，　　〔蒸平〕　[106]

94

Thus, the person who has attained *dao* is weak of purpose[61] yet
  forceful in action; [100]

> His heart is empty yet his response to things is always as it
>   should be. [100]
> What is meant by being "weak of purpose" is:
> Being pliant and placid,
> He takes his refuge in the timorous
> And pursues his actions in what cannot be done; [101]
> Serenely without thoughts for the morrow
> He never anticipates the opportune moment, [101]
> And freewheeling, he never goes against the myriad things;
> Never taking the lead
> He responds only when stimulated. [101]

Hence, the exalted necessarily takes the lowly as title,

> And the lofty necessarily takes the base as
>   foundation.[62] [101]
> It means lodging in the small to encompass the
>   large, [102]
> Dwelling in the central to regulate the peripheral, [102]
> Practicing the pliant yet achieving the unbending, [103]
> Exercising the weak yet attaining the strong. [103]
> Transforming and setting in motion, [104]
> And attaining *dao* of the One,
> He is able to rectify the many by using the few. [104]
> What is meant by "forceful in action" is:
> In responding to the unforeseen in an emergency [105]
> And warding off adversities, [105]
> There is nothing his strength cannot overcome, [106]
> And there is no enemy that he cannot get on top
>   of. [106]

應化揆時，　　〔之平〕　　[107]
莫能害之。　　〔之平〕　　[107]

是故欲剛者必以柔守之，　　〔幽上〕　　[108]
欲強者必以弱保之。　　〔幽上〕　　[108]
積於柔則剛，　　〔陽平〕　　[109]
積於弱則強，　　〔陽平〕　　[109]
觀其所積，
以知禍福之鄉。　　〔陽平〕　　[109]
強勝不若己者，
至於若己者而同；　　〔東平〕　　[109]
柔勝出於己者，
其力不可量。　　〔陽平〕　　[109]
故兵強則滅，　　〔月〕　　[110]
木強則折，　　〔月〕　　[110]
革堅則裂，　　〔月〕　　[110]
齒堅於舌　　〔月〕　　[110]
而先之弊。　　〔祭〕　　[110]
是故柔弱者、生之榦[16]也，　　〔元平〕　　[111] [A]
（而）堅強者、死之徒也。　　〔魚平〕　　[112] [A]
先唱[17]者、窮之路也，　　〔魚去〕　　[112] [A]
後動者、達之原也。　　〔元平〕　　[111] [A]

96

In responding to the workings of transformation he
gauges the most opportune moment [107]
And nothing is able to obstruct him. [107]

Hence, those who want to be unbending necessarily watch over it by
pliancy, [108]
And those who want to be strong necessarily guard it
by weakness. [108]
The accumulation of pliancy results in
unbendingness [109]
And the accumulation of weakness results in
strength; [109]
Observe what is being accumulated,
And you will know which direction it is heading for:
fortune or calamity. [109]
Strength overcomes that which is inferior to itself;
When it comes to its equal there will be a draw. [109]
Weakness overcomes that which is superior to itself,
Its might being immeasurable. [109]
Thus, a weapon that is unyielding will break; [110]
A piece of wood that is stiff will snap; [110]
A piece of leather that is hard will split. [110]
The teeth being harder than the tongue [110]
Are the first to wear out. [110]
Hence, the pliant and the weak are the trunk of life, [111]
While the hard and strong are the companions of
death.[63] [112]
To sing the lead is the road to a dead end, [112]
Whereas to follow behind in making a move is the
source of winning through.[64] [111]

何以知其然也？凡人、中壽七十歲，然而趣舍指湊，日以
（自）〔月〕悔也，以至於死，故蘧伯玉年五十而有四十九年
非。何者？

先者難爲知，
而後者易爲攻也。
先者上高，
則後者攀之；　　〔元平〕　[113]
先者（論）〔踰〕下，
則後者（蹶）〔躐〕之；　〔元上〕　[113]
先者隤陷，
則後者以謀；　　〔之平〕　[114]
先者敗績，
則後者（逢）〔違〕之。　〔之平〕　[114]

由此觀之，先者，則後者之弓矢質的也。

猶錞之與刃，刃犯難　〔元去〕　[115] [A]
而錞無患者，　　〔元去〕　[115] [A]
何也？
以其託於後位，　〔微去〕　[116] [A]
〔有所屏蔽〕也。　〔祭〕　[116] [A]
此俗世庸民之所公見也，
而賢知者弗能避也。

98

How do we know this is the case? The average lifespan of man is seventy years, but with all our choices and goals, we regret every day what we did the day before and in this way we reach the end of our life. Thus, Qu Boyu, at fifty years of age, realized that he was wrong at forty-nine.[65] Why?

> It is difficult for the person taking the lead to be wise,
> While it is easy for the one coming behind to achieve results.
> When a person who leads the way climbs to a high place,
> The one coming behind hoists himself up by grabbing onto
>   him; [113]
> When the person who leads the way steps over gaps on the
>   way down,
> The one coming behind treads on him as a stepping-stone; [113]
> When the person who leads the way stumbles and falls into a
>   hole,
> The one coming behind takes counsel; [114]
> When the person who leads the way is routed,
> The one coming behind turns his back on him. [114]

Viewing it from this perspective, the person who leads the way is the target which attracts the arrows, taking them away from those coming behind.

> It is like the difference between the butt end of a weapon
>   shaft and the blade. The blade braves danger [115]
> While the butt end of the shaft is at no risk. [115]
> Why?
> It is thanks to the rear position the butt end occupies, [116]
> Which is screened and covered. [116]
> This is a truth open to the view of even the most ordinary
>   man
> Yet the superior and wise are never able to act on it.[66]

所謂後者，非謂其底滯而不發，凝竭而不流，貴其周於數而合於時也。夫執道理以耦變，先亦制後，後亦制先。是何則？不失其所以制人，人不能制也。

時之反側，　　〔職〕　　[117]

閒不容息，　　〔職〕　　[117]

先之則大過，　〔歌去〕　[118]　[A]

後之則不逮。　〔微去〕　[118]　[A]

夫日回而月周，〔幽平〕　[119]

時不與人游，　〔幽平〕　[119]

故聖人不貴尺之璧，

而重寸之陰，時難得而易失也。

禹之趨時也，

履遺而弗取，　〔魚上〕　[120]　[A]

冠挂而弗顧，　〔魚去〕　[120]　[A]

非爭其先也，而爭其得時也。

是故聖人守清道而抱雌節，

因循應變，　　〔元去〕　[121]　[A]

常後而不先。　〔諄去〕　[121]　[A]

柔弱以靜，　　〔耕去〕　[122]

舒安以定，　　〔耕去〕　[122]

攻大礦堅，　　〔元平〕　[123]　[A]

莫能與之爭〔先〕[18]。　〔元平〕　[123]　[A]

By "coming behind" is not meant being stagnant, numb, and inert. Rather, it means putting store in always being in accord with that which is necessarily so, and being appropriate to the moment. When a person grasps the principles of *dao* and uses them to match change, then he controls others whether he is in the lead or in the rear. Why is this? Because he does not let go of the means to control others, giving others no chance of controlling him.

Section 13

> The right moment becomes the wrong [117]
> Before one can take a breath. [117]
> One who acts too soon anticipates the opportunity, [118]
> And one who acts too late gets left behind. [118]
> The sun revolves, the moon wheels its course, [119]
> And the right moment waits for no man. [119]
> Thus, the sage values an inch of time over a foot of precious
>   jade.
> It is because the right moment is so hard to catch and so easy
>   to miss.
> When Yu was in hot pursuit of the critical moment,
> He would not stop to pick up a sandal that had slipped off [120]
> Or look back after a snagged cap. [120]
> It was not that he was vying to get ahead of others, but rather
>   that he was vying to catch the right moment.

Hence, the sage abides by the limpid *dao* and embraces the principle of femininity.

> In taking advantage of what is already there and in responding
>   to change, [121]
> He always stays in the rear and does not take the lead. [121]
> Pliant and weak, he is calm; [122]
> Relaxed and peaceful, he is poised. [122]
> But in assailing the big or grinding down the hard, [123]
> There are none that can vie with him for the lead. [123]

天下之物，莫柔弱於水，

        然而大不可極，   〔職〕   [124]

          深不可測，   〔職〕   [124]

        脩極於無窮，

遠（渝）〔淪〕於無崖，   〔支平〕   [125]

         息耗減益，

          通於不訾，   〔支平〕   [125]

       上天則爲雨露，   〔魚去〕   [126]

       下地則爲潤澤，   〔鐸〕   [126]

       萬物弗得不生，   〔耕平〕   [127]

       百事不得不成，   〔耕平〕   [127]

         大包群生

而無（好憎）〔私好〕，   〔幽去〕   [128]

         澤及蚑蟯

          而不求報，   〔幽去〕   [128]

     富贍天下而不既，   〔微去〕   [129]

     德施百姓而不費，   〔微去〕   [129]

行（而）不可得〔而〕窮極也，   〔職〕   [130]

微（而）不可得〔而〕把握也，   〔屋〕   [130]

          擊之無創，   〔陽平〕   [131]

          刺之不傷，   〔陽平〕   [131]

          斬之不斷，   〔元去〕   [132]

          焚之不然，   〔元平〕   [132]

       淖溺流遁[19]，   〔諄去〕   [133]

          錯繆相紛   〔諄平〕   [133]

        而不可靡散，   〔元去〕   [132]

          利貫金石，

          强濟天下，   〔魚上〕   [134]

In the world there is nothing more pliant and weak than water
> And yet it is great beyond reckoning [124]
> And deep beyond fathoming.[67] [124]
> In length it ends only in the interminable
> And in distance it merges into the boundless; [125]
> Waxing and waning, increasing and decreasing,
> It runs into the incalculable. [125]
> Going up to the heavens it becomes rain and dew; [126]
> Going down to the earth it becomes moisture. [126]
> The myriad things cannot be produced without it, [127]
> And the events of the world cannot culminate without it. [127]
> With its magnitude embracing all living creatures,
> It is without private likes; [128]
> With its beneficence extending even to the paltry insects,
> It is not after gratitude. [128]
> Having given to the world it is nevertheless not exhausted in
>   its riches; [129]
> Having bestowed on the people it finds this to have cost
>   nothing to its bounty. [129]
> It is ever flowing yet we can never see it reaching its end; [130]
> It is minute yet we can never hold it in our grasp. [130]
> Strike it and you will not wound it; [131]
> Stab it and you will not injure it; [131]
> Hack at it and you will not sever it; [132]
> Put fire to it and you will not burn it. [132]
> Being fluid it flows and follows its own inclinations; [133]
> Mixing and coalescing, [133]
> It cannot be divided up. [132]
> Its sharpness is such that it can penetrate metal and stone;
> Its strength is such that it can give succor to the entire
>   world. [134]

動溶無形之域，
而翺翔忽區之上，
邅回川谷之閒，
而滔騰大荒之野，　　〔魚上〕　[134]
有餘不足，
與天地取與，　　　　〔魚上〕　[134]
授萬物而無所前後，　〔魚上〕　[134]

是故無所私而無所公，〔東平〕　[135]
靡濫振蕩，
與天地鴻洞，　　　　〔東平〕　[135]
無所左而無所右，　　〔之上〕　[136]
蟠委錯紾，
與萬物（始終）〔終始〕，〔之上〕　[136]
是謂至德。

　　夫水所以能成其至德於天下者，以其淖溺潤滑也。故老聃
之言曰：「天下至柔，馳騁於天下之至堅。出於無有，入於無
閒。吾是以知無爲之有益。」夫無形者，物之大祖也；無音
者，聲之大宗也。其子爲光，其孫爲水，皆生於〔無〕形乎！
　　夫光可見而不可握，
　　水可循而不可毀，　〔微上〕　[137] [A]
　　故有像之類，　　　〔微去〕　[137] [A]
　　莫尊於水。　　　　〔微上〕　[137] [A]
出生入死，自無蹠有，自有蹠無，而以衰賤矣。

104

It moves into the realm of the formless
And soars above the elusive and ethereal;
It meanders through the river valleys
And swells over into the vast wilderness. [134]
In its abundance and insufficiency
It allows the world to take from and to give to it, [134]
Dispensing to the myriad things without favoring anyone. [134]

Hence, without distinction between private and public [135]
It inundates with a thunderous roar,
Forming one vast expanse with the universe; [135]
Veering neither left nor right [136]
It circulates and mingles,
And has its beginning and end together with the myriad
things. [136]
This is called supremely excellent (de).

The reason that water is able to attain supreme de in the world
is because it is moist and lubricious. Thus, the teachings of Lao Dan
state: "The most pliant substance in the universe rides roughshod
over the hardest. Emerging from that which is without substance, it
enters that which is without seam. Thus, I know the advantage of
'nonaction.'"[68] The formless is the great ancestor of things, and the
soundless is the great progenitor of the audible. Light is the son and
water is the grandson of the formless, and both are born out of it.

Light can be seen but not grasped;
Water can be stroked but not be destroyed. [137]
Thus, among things that can be delineated, [137]
None occupies a position more exalted than water. [137]
"Coming out means life and going in means death"[69] is taking
the step from nonbeing into being, and then from being back into
nonbeing, and having done so, the first step towards decline into
baseness has been taken.

是故清靜者，德之至也；而柔弱者，道之要也；虛（而）
〔無〕恬愉者，萬物之用也。肅然應感，殷然反本，則淪於無
形矣。所謂無形者，一之謂也。所謂一者，無匹合於天下者
也。

卓然獨立，

塊然獨處，　　〔魚上〕　[138]

上通九天，

下貫九野，　　〔魚上〕　[138]

員不中規，

方不中矩，　　〔魚上〕　[138]

大渾而爲一，

葉累而無根，　　〔諄平〕　[139]

懷囊天地，

爲道關門，　　〔諄平〕　[139]

穆忞隱閔，

純德獨存，　　〔諄平〕　[139]

布施而不既，

用之而不勤。　　〔諄平〕　[139]

是故視之不見其形，　〔耕平〕　[140]

聽之不聞其聲，　〔耕平〕　[140]

循之不得其身，　〔眞平〕　[140]

無形而有形生焉，　〔耕平〕　[141]

無聲而五音鳴焉，　〔耕平〕　[141]

無味而五味形焉，　〔耕平〕　[141]

無色而五色成焉。　〔耕平〕　[141]

是故有生於無，　〔魚平〕　[142]

實出於虛，　〔魚平〕　[142]

天下爲之圈，

則名實同居。　　〔魚平〕　[142]

Hence, limpidity and tranquillity are the acme of *de*, pliancy and weakness are at the nub of *dao*, and vacuity and serenity are the use of the myriad things. Where a person solemnly responds to what is encountered and in his fullness returns to the root, he has entered the realm of the formless. By the "formless" is meant the "one," and by the "one" is meant that which has no peer in the world.

> Alone, it stands head and shoulders above others;
> Like a clod of earth existing apart [138]
> It reaches the nine celestial fields above
> And ranges over the nine divisions of territory below.[70] [138]
> Though round, it does not accord with the compass,
> And though square, it does not accord with the carpenter's
>   square. [138]
> It constitutes "one" out of a massive conglomeration;
> It is leaves piled on without roots. [139]
> Pocketing the cosmos,
> It is the bar that shuts the *dao* behind the gate. [139]
> Unformed and shapeless,
> Its pure *de* alone exists. [139]
> It constantly dispenses abroad yet is never penurious;
> It is constantly used yet is never exhausted.[71] [139]
> Hence, look at it, and you do not see its form; [140]
> Listen to it, and you do not hear its sound; [140]
> Stroke it and you do not catch hold of its body.[72] [140]
> It is formless yet things with form are born therefrom; [141]
> It is soundless yet the five notes arise therefrom; [141]
> It is tasteless yet the five flavors take form therefrom; [141]
> It is colorless yet the five colors emerge therefrom. [141]
> Hence, since being is born out of nonbeing [142]
> And the full comes out of the empty, [142]
> Having the world as their corral,
> Name and reality dwell together. [142]

音之數不過五，而五音之變不可勝聽也。味之和不過五，
而五味之化不可勝嘗也。色之數不過五，而五色之變不可勝觀
也。

故音者，宮立而五音形矣；　〔耕平〕　[143]

味者，甘立而五味亭矣；　〔耕平〕　[143]

色者，白立而五色成矣；　〔耕平〕　[143]

道者，一立而萬物生矣。　〔耕平〕　[143]

是故一之理，　〔之上〕　[144]

施四海；　〔之上〕　[144]

一之解，　〔支上〕　[145]

際天地[20]。　〔支去〕　[145]

其全也，　〔元平〕　[146] [A]

純〔諄平〕兮若樸；　〔屋〕　[147] [A]

其散也，　〔元平〕　[146] [A]

混〔諄平〕[21]兮若濁。　〔屋〕　[147] [A]

濁而徐清，　〔耕平〕　[148]

沖而徐盈，　〔耕平〕　[148]

澹兮其若深淵，　〔眞平〕　[149]

汎兮其若浮雲，　〔諄平〕　[149]

若無而有，

若亡而存。　〔諄平〕　[149]

萬物之總，　〔東上〕　[150]

皆閱一孔；　〔東上〕　[150]

百事之根，　〔諄平〕　[151]

皆出一門。　〔諄平〕　[151]

The number of notes is no more than five yet the variations on these five notes are more than one's ear can ever listen to; the number of flavors is no more than five yet the permutations of these five flavors are more than one's tongue can ever savor; the number of colors is no more than five yet the mutations of these five colors are more than one's eyes can ever feast upon.

· Thus, in music, once the *gong* note is established the five notes become manifest. [143]

Where taste is concerned, once sweetness is established the five flavors are fixed. [143]

And for colors, once white is established the range of the five colors is produced. [143]

Similarly with *dao*, once the "one" is established the myriad things come to be. [143]

Hence, when the "one" is disentangled [144]

It can be dealt out to the four seas, [144]

And when the "one" is unraveled [145]

It will reach the limits of heaven and earth. [145]

In its wholeness, it is pure, [146]

Like the uncarved jade; [147]

In its dispersion, it is chaotic, [146]

Like murky water. [147]

From being murky, it slowly becomes limpid; [148]

From being empty, it slowly becomes full.[73] [148]

Being settled, it is like deep waters;[74] [149]

Being buoyant, it is like floating clouds. [149]

It seems not to be there yet is there;

It seems to be gone yet is still there. [149]

The convergence of the myriad things [150]

Goes through a single aperture; [150]

The roots of the various happenings [151]

All issue forth from a single gateway. [151]

其動無形，

變化若神；　　〔眞平〕　[151]

其行無迹，

常後而先。　　〔諄平〕　[151]

是故至人之治也，

掩其聰明，　　〔陽平〕　[152]

滅其文章，　　〔陽平〕　[152]

依道廢智，

與民同出于公。　〔東平〕　[152]

去其誘慕，　　〔魚去〕　[153]

除其嗜欲，

（損）〔捐〕其思慮。　〔魚去〕　[153]

約其所守則（察）〔塞〕[22]，　〔職〕　[154] [Tb]

寡其所求則得。　　〔職〕　[154] [Tb]

夫任耳目以聽視者，

勞形而不明；　　〔陽平〕　[155]

以知慮爲治者，

苦心而無功。　　〔東平〕　[155]

是故聖人一度循軌，

不變其宜，

不易其常，　　〔陽平〕　[155]

放準（修）〔循〕繩，

曲因其當。　　〔陽平〕　[155]

夫喜怒者，道之邪也；憂悲者，德之失也；好憎者，心之
過也；嗜欲者，性之累也。

人大怒破陰，　　〔侵平〕　[156]

大喜墜陽；　　〔陽平〕　[157]

Its movements are hidden from sight

And its changes and transformations are godlike; [151]

It does not leave any traces behind in its progress;

It is ever in the lead though always coming behind. [151]

Hence, in his governance, the surpassing person:

Covers up his perspicacity [152]

And smothers his outward embellishments. [152]

He puts aside cleverness and follows *dao*;

Together with the people he goes along the path of
  impartiality. [152]

He sets aside all yearnings, [153]

Abandons all desires,

And does away with all deliberation. [153]

Since he reduces to essentials what he abides by, he is
  discerning; [154]

Since he curtails what he seeks, he gets it. [154]

Those who rely on their eyes and ears to see and hear

Tire out their persons yet fail to see or hear things clearly; [155]

Those who govern through cleverness and deliberation

Toil their minds yet achieve nothing. [155]

Hence, the sage follows the course of the one norm.

He does not change what is suitable to it

Or alter what is constant. [155]

Following the water gauge and adhering to the plumb line,

He does in every way what is fitting to the circumstances. [155]

Section 16

Gladness and anger are a deviation from *dao*; worry and sorrow
are a falling from *de*; likes and dislikes are excesses of the heart;
cravings and desires are a burden on the nature.[75]

In man, a great anger shatters the *yin* [156]

While great gladness weighs down the *yang*. [157]

薄氣發瘖，　　　〔侵平〕　[156]
驚怖爲狂；　　　〔陽平〕　[157]
憂悲多恚，　　　〔錫〕　　[158]
病乃成積；　　　〔錫〕　　[158]
好憎繁多，　　　〔歌平〕　[159]
禍乃相隨。　　　〔歌平〕　[159]

故心不憂樂，德之至也；通而不變，靜之至也；嗜欲不載，虛之至也；無所好憎，平之至也；不與物（散）〔殽〕，粹之至也。能此五者，則通於神明。通於神明者，得其內者也。

是故以中制外，　　〔祭〕　　[160]
百事不廢；　　　〔祭〕　　[160]
中能得之，　　　〔職〕　　[161]
則外能（收）〔牧〕之。〔職〕　[161]
中之得，
則五藏寧，　　　〔耕平〕　[162]
思慮平，　　　　〔耕平〕　[162]
筋力勁强，　　　〔陽平〕　[163]
耳目聰明，　　　〔陽平〕　[163]
疏達而不悖，　　〔微去〕　[164] [A]
堅强而不鞼，　　〔微去〕　[164] [A]
無所大過，　　　〔歌去〕　[164] [A]
而無所不逮，　　〔微去〕　[164] [A]
處小而不逼，
處大而不窕，　　〔宵上〕　[165]

112

> *Yin* and *yang* approaching each other gives rise to
> dumbness [156]
> And alarm and fear bring on madness.[76] [157]
> Where there is worry, sorrow, and much rage, [158]
> Illness will accrue; [158]
> Where likes and dislikes proliferate, [159]
> Calamities are sure to follow. [159]

Thus, being free from worry or joy is the acme of *de*; being
unblocked yet not changing is the acme of tranquillity; carrying no
freight of cravings or desires is the acme of vacuity; being free of all
likes and dislikes is the acme of equanimity; not to be admixed with
external things is the acme of purity.[77] If one is able to keep these five
intact, he will commune with the spirits, and one who communes
with the spirits finds it within himself.

Hence, if one regulates the external from the core of his person, [160]
> His various affairs will not end in failure. [160]
> If he gets it at the core, [161]
> He can nurture externals. [161]
> Getting it at the core,
> Will mean his five viscera will be calm, [162]
> Reflection and deliberation will be stilled, [162]
> His body's sinews and muscles will be strong, [163]
> And his eyes and ears will be perspicacious. [163]
> Freely intercommunicating in his mind, he is without
> contradictions; [164]
> He is hardy and strong without snapping. [164]
> He will be free of both excesses [164]
> And deficiencies. [164]
> He dwells in the small without finding it too cramped;
> He dwells in the large without finding it overspacious. [165]

其魂不躁，

其神不嬈，　　〔宵上〕　[165]

湫漻寂漠，

爲天下梟。　　〔宵平〕　[165]

（迫）〔感〕則能應，　〔蒸去〕　[166]

（感）〔迫〕則能動；　〔東上〕　[166]

物穆無窮，

變無形像。　　〔陽上〕　[167]

優游委縱，

如響之與景；　〔陽上〕　[167]

登高臨下，

無失所秉；　　〔陽上〕　[167]

履危行險，

無忘玄伏。　　〔陽上〕　[167]

大道坦坦，

去身不遠，　　〔元上〕　[168] [A]

求之近者，　　〔諄上〕　[168] [A]

往而復反，　　〔元上〕　[168] [A]

能存之此，

其德不虧，　　〔歌平〕　[169]

萬物紛糅，

與之轉化[23]，　〔歌去〕　[169]

以聽天下，

若背風而馳，　〔歌平〕　[169]

是謂至德。

至德則樂矣。

古之人有居巖穴

而神不遺者，　〔微平〕　[170]

末世有勢爲萬乘

而日憂悲者。　〔微平〕　[170]

114

His soul is not agitated
Nor is his spirit troubled. [165]
Composed and serene,
He becomes cock of the walk. [165]
Up against external things, he is able to respond, [166]
Borne down upon, he is able to move. [166]
Without form and without end,
In his changes he is without visible shape. [167]
He stretches and bends along with things,
Like an echo or a shadow. [167]
Even when looking down over a precipice,
He does not lose what he holds on to; [167]
Traveling amid perils and dangers
He does not forget his dark crutch.[78] [167]
(The *dao*, being ubiquitous
Is not far removed from one's person. [168]
One who seeks a thing near at hand, [168]
Having gone on, it is sure to return.)[79] [168]
If he is able to retain it there,
His *de* is not dented. [169]
With the myriad things which are chaotic and embroiled,
He responds to them in turn with transformation [169]
In order to listen to the world.
This is like galloping along with a tailwind. [169]
This is called the acme of *de*.
And having reached the acme of *de*, he will be in a state
    of joy.

Among the ancients there were those who, dwelling in rocky
    grottos, did not feel at a loss in their spirits, [170]
While in periods of decline, there were those who, ruling ten-
    thousand-chariot states, hardly passed a day without
    worry and sorrow. [170]

由此觀之，聖亡乎治人，而在于得道；樂亡于富貴，而在于德和。知大己而小天下，則幾於道矣。

所謂樂者，豈必處京臺、章華，游雲夢、沙丘，耳聽《九韶》、《六瑩》。口味煎熬芬芳，馳騁夷道，釣射鶬鵝之謂樂乎？吾所謂樂者，人得其得者。

夫得其得者，
不以奢爲樂，
不以廉[24]爲悲，　　〔微平〕　[171]
與陰俱閉，
與陽俱開。　　〔微平〕　[171]
故子夏心戰而（臞）〔臞〕，
（得）道〔勝〕而肥。　〔微平〕　[171]

聖人不以身役物，　〔術〕　[172] [A]
不以欲滑和，
是故其爲（曜）〔樂〕不忻忻，
其爲悲不惵惵，　　〔月〕　[172] [A]
萬方百變，　　〔元去〕　[173]
消搖而無所定，　　〔耕去〕　[173]
吾獨忼慨遺物，　　〔術〕　[172]
而與道同出。　〔術〕　[172]

Viewing it from this perspective, sagacity lies not in governing others, but rather in getting hold of *dao*; joy lies not in wealth and rank, but rather in gaining the symphonious. If one knows how to look upon himself as large and the world as small, he is close to *dao*.

As for what is called "joy," surely it need not necessarily be residing in the Jing pavilion or Zhanghua, making excursions to the Yunmeng lake or the Shaqiu tower, listening to the Jiushao or Liuying music, tasting the savory and aromatic, galloping along a smooth and even highway, or hunting and shooting down the phoenix. What I call "joy" is a person getting what is to be got within himself.

> Now, "getting what is to be got within himself"
>> Is not taking luxury as joy,
>> And not taking straitened circumstances as
>>> sorrow. [171]
>> He closes as the *yin* closes
>> And opens as the *yang* opens. [171]

Thus, Zixia grew gaunt with inner conflict,
> But grew rotund when *dao* gained the upper hand.[80] [171]

> The sage does not make his person a slave to external
>> things [172]
> Nor does he allow desire to disturb his symphoniousness.

Hence, he is not elated with joy,
> Nor downcast with sorrow. [172]
> In the innumerable different directions there are countless
>> changes, [173]
> Untrammeled I am in no fixed position. [173]
> I alone am in great spirits, and leaving things behind, [172]
> Travel along the same path as *dao*.[81] [172]

117

是故有以自得〔也〕，喬木之下，

空穴之中，

足以適情。　〔耕平〕　　[174]

無以自得也，

雖以天下爲家，

萬民爲臣妾，

不足以養生也。　〔耕平〕　　[174]

能至于無樂者，則無不樂；無不樂則至（極樂）〔樂極〕矣。

夫建鍾鼓，列管弦，席旃茵，傅旄象，耳聽朝歌北鄙靡靡之樂，齊靡曼之色，陳酒行觴，夜以繼日，强弩（于）〔干〕高鳥，走犬（遂）〔逐〕狡兔，此其爲樂也，炎炎赫赫，忧然若有所誘慕。解車休馬，罷酒徹樂，

而心忽然若有所喪，　〔陽平〕　　[175]

悵然若有所亡也。　〔陽平〕　　[175]

是何則？

不以內樂外，　〔祭〕　　[176] [A]

而以外樂內，　〔微去〕　　[176] [A]

樂作而喜，

曲終而悲，　〔微去〕　　[176] [A]

悲喜轉而相生，　〔耕平〕　　[177]

精神亂營，　〔耕平〕　　[177]

不得須臾平。　〔耕平〕　　[177]

Hence, when a person has the means to find it in himself,

> Even under a tall tree or in an empty cave,
>
> His real nature will be able to find satisfaction. [174]
>
> If he does not have the means to find it in himself,
>
> Even if he has the empire as his personal possession
>
> And the myriad people as his subjects,
>
> This will not be sufficient to give his vitality sustenance. [174]

If a man can get to a state in which there is nothing which he enjoys, there will be nothing he does not enjoy; when there is nothing he does not enjoy, he has then reached the extremity of the highest joy.

Section 17

Setting out the bells and drums, putting the winds and strings out in lines, laying down mats of woolen fabric, decorating banners and ivory ornaments, listening to the delicate and melancholy music of Zhaoke and Beibi, lining up girls of beautiful complexion, laying on the wine and passing the goblet round and reveling night and day, powerful crossbows shooting at high-flying birds and running dogs in pursuit of a crafty rabbit—these things being regarded as joy under the hot sun—it is as if there was something one was yearning after. When they unhitch the vehicles, unharness the horses, put an end to the drinking, and clear away the musical instruments,

> Vaguely they feel as if something is missing [175]
>
> Or as if pining after something lost. [175]
>
> Why is this?
>
> Because not looking for the inward to please the external, [176]
>
> They were pleasing the inward with the external. [176]
>
> When the music starts, they feel happy,
>
> But when the performance is over, they are sad. [176]
>
> With happiness and sadness giving rise alternately to one
> > another, [177]
>
> The spirit is thrown into turmoil [177]
>
> And cannot find a moment's peace. [177]

察其所以，不得其形， 〔耕平〕 [177]

而日以傷生， 〔耕平〕 [177]

失其得者也。

是故內不得於中，稟授於外而以自飾也，

不浸于肌膚，

不浹于骨髓，

不留于心志， 〔之去〕 [178] [A]

不滯于五藏。 〔陽平〕 [179] [A]

故從外入者，

無主於中不止。 〔之上〕 [178] [A]

從中出者，

無應於外不行。 〔陽平〕 [179] [A]

If we seek for the cause behind this, we cannot get a hold of
it, [177]

Yet this is doing injury daily to one's vitality, [177]

And failing to secure what is to be got.

Hence, failing to find it within oneself, one takes some external thing
and uses it for ornament.

It does not penetrate even one's skin,

It does not permeate one's bones and marrow,

It does not settle in one's heart [178]

And does not stay in the five viscera. [179]

Thus, what comes in from the outside

Will not stop inside unless it finds a host. [178]

What issues forth from inside

Will not prevail unless there is response from the
outside.[82] [179]

故聽善言便計，雖愚者（和）〔知〕說之；稱至德高行，雖不肖者知慕之。說之者衆而用之者鮮，慕之者多而行之者寡。所以然者，何也？不能反諸性也。夫內不開於中而强學問者，（不）入於耳而不著於心。此何以異於聾者之歌也？效人爲之而無以自樂也，聲出於口則越而散矣。夫心者，五藏之主也，所以制使四支，流行血氣，馳騁于是非之境，而出入于百事之門戶者也。是故不得於心而有經天下之氣，是猶無耳而欲調鍾鼓，無目而欲喜文章也，亦必不勝其任矣。

故天下神器，不可爲也，

　　　　　　爲者敗之，　　　〔祭〕　　　[180]

　　　　　　執者失之[25]。　　〔質〕　　　[180]

夫許由小天下而不以己易堯者，志遺于天下。所以然者，何也？因天下而爲天下也。

　　　　　　天下之要，

　　　不（任）〔在〕於彼　　　〔歌上〕　　[181]

　　　　　　而在於我，　　　〔歌上〕　　[181]

Thus, on hearing good advice or sound counsel, even an idiot knows enough to be taken by it; where the highest *de* and lofty conduct are held forth as examples, even an unworthy person will know to want to emulate it. Those who are taken by it are numerous, but those who can actually adopt it are rare; those who are attracted by it are many, but those who can actually put it into practice are few. Why is this so? Because they are unable to look inward and find it in their own nature. For one who insists on learning while being internally unreceptive, what is taught neither enters the ears nor registers on the mind.[83] How is this different from a deaf person trying to sing? All he does is copy what others do while all the time lacking the means to delight himself; the moment the notes come out his mouth, they are lost to the empty air. The heart is the ruler of the five viscera; it is responsible for regulating and engaging the four limbs, circulating the blood and *qi*, galloping about in the realm of right and wrong, and going in and out of the gateway from which the various affairs of the world issue. Hence, for a man to have the ambition to manage the world while not finding it in his own heart is like a person without ears trying to tune the bells and drums, or a man without eyes wanting to take delight in colors and designs. He is sure to be unequal to the task.

Section 18

Thus, "the empire is a sacred vessel, and cannot be deliberately managed.

>> To manage it is to spoil it; [180]

>> To grasp it is to lose it."[84] [180]

> That Xu You belittled the empire and would not change places with Yao was because the empire did not figure in what he was intent upon. Why was this so? Because he was of the mind that the empire should be managed by taking it for what it is.[85]

>> The essence of the empire

>> Lies not with it [181]

>> But with me; [181]

123

不在於人　　　〔眞平〕　[182]

而在於（我）身，　〔眞平〕　[182]

　　身得　　　　〔職〕　　[183] [A]

　　則萬物備矣。　〔之去〕　[183] [A]

徵於心術之論，則嗜欲好憎外（失）〔矣〕。

是故無所喜而無所怒，　〔魚上〕　[184]

無所樂而無所苦，　〔魚上〕　[184]

萬物玄同（也），

　　無非無是，　〔脂上〕　[185]

　　化育玄燿，

　　生而如死。　〔脂上〕　[185]

夫天下者亦吾有也，吾亦天下之有也，天下之與我，豈有
間哉！夫有天下者，豈必攝權持勢，操殺生之柄而以行其號令
（邪）〔哉〕？吾所謂有天下者，非謂此也，自得而已。自
得，則天下亦得我矣。吾與天下相得，則常相有已，又焉有
（不）得容其間者乎！

所謂自得者，全其身者也。全其身，則與道爲一矣。

　　故雖游於江潯海裔，　〔祭〕　[186]

　　馳要裏，

　　建翠蓋，　　〔祭〕　[186]

Lies not in others [182]

But in my person. [182]

Once one's person is gained, [183]

The full complement of the myriad things will follow. [183]

Once one understands the theory about the way of the heart, then desires, likes, and dislikes all become extraneous.

Hence, there is nothing one is pleased with, there is nothing one gets angry about, [184]

There is nothing one finds enjoyment in, there is nothing one finds hardship in. [184]

The myriad things merge in mysterious unity:

Without right or wrong, [185]

In a bedazzling transformation,

Life is like death. [185]

Section 19

The empire is something which I possess, while I am also something which the empire possesses. How could there be any gap between the empire and me? Why must "possessing the empire" mean effecting one's edicts and commands by holding authority and power and wielding the handle of life and death? By "possessing the empire" is not meant this, but simply finding it in oneself. If I find it in myself then the empire also finds me in it. If the empire and I find it in each other, then we will always possess each other. Again, how can there be room for anything to be wedged between the empire and me?

"Finding it in oneself" is to preserve oneself intact, and when one preserves himself intact, he is one with *dao*.

Thus, roaming along the riverbanks and seashores, [186]

Galloping along with the fine Yaoniao horse in harness

And a kingfisher-feathered canopy overhead, [186]

目觀《掉羽》、《武象》之樂，
　　　耳聽滔朗奇麗激抮之音，　　〔侵平〕　　[187]
　　　揚鄭、衛之浩樂，
　　　結激楚之遺風，　　　　　　〔侵平〕　　[187]
　　射沼[26]濱之高鳥，　　　　　〔幽上〕　　[188]
　　　逐苑囿之走獸，　　　　　　〔幽上〕　　[188]
此齊民之所以淫泆流湎，聖人處之，不足以營其精神，亂
其氣志，使心怵然失其情性。

　　　　　處窮僻之鄉，
　　　　　側谿谷之間，
　　　　隱于榛薄之中，
　　　　　環堵之室，
　　　　　茨之以生茅，　　　　　〔幽平〕　　[189]
　　　　　蓬戶甕牖，
　　　　　揉桑以為樞，　　　　　〔魚平〕　　[189]
　　　　　上漏下溼，
　　　　　潤浸北房，　　　　　　〔陽平〕　　[190]
　　　　　雪霜滾灖，
　　　　　浸潭苽蔣，　　　　　　〔陽平〕　　[190]
　　　逍遙于廣澤之中，
而仿洋于山（峽）〔岬〕之旁，　　〔陽平〕　　[190]

Watching the traditional *diaoyu* feather dance and the
    wuxiang dance,
Listening to elegant, graceful, and euphonic musical
    performances, [187]
Playing the popular and sensuous music of Zheng and Wey,
Joining in the rousing ballads of Chu's past glories, [187]
Shooting high-flying birds in the marshlands, [188]
And giving chase to running game in hunting preserves— [188]
These are things which the common run of men will indulge
themselves in wantonly and without any sense of proper measure. In
similar circumstances, a sage would not find it worthy for his spirit to
be perplexed by such things, his purposes to be confused, or his mind
to be led astray from his original nature.

A dwelling in a remote village
Wedged amongst gorges and valleys,
A little shanty shack
Hidden amongst thick growth and underbrush,
With a thatched roof of grass, [189]
A woven sagebrush door,
Pots for windows
And bent mulberrry twigs for door hinges, [189]
A shack with leaky roof and puddles on the floor,
Wherein the damp creeps into the northern quarters [190]
And into which the snow and frost seeps,
Soaking the grass matting, [190]
And then nearby roaming about in the vast expanses of
    marshland
And the mountain valleys— [190]

此齊民之所爲形植（藜）〔黎〕（累）〔黑〕，憂悲而不得志也，聖人處之，不爲愁悴怨（愍）〔慰〕而（不）失其所以自樂也。是何（也）則？內有以通于天機，而不以貴賤貧富勞逸失其志德者也。

故夫烏之啞啞，　　〔鐸〕　　[191]
鵲之唶唶，　　〔鐸〕　　[191]

豈嘗爲寒暑燥溼變其聲哉！是故夫得道已定，而不待萬物之推移也，非以一時之變化而定吾所以自得也。吾所謂得者，性命之情，處其所安也。夫性命者，與形俱出其宗，

形備而性命成，　　〔耕平〕　　[192]
性命成而好憎生矣。　　〔耕平〕　　[192]

故士有一定之論，女有不易之行，規矩不能方圓，鉤繩不能曲直。天地之永，登丘不可爲脩，居卑不可爲短。是故得道者，

窮而不懾，
達而不榮，　　〔耕平〕　　[193]

This is a situation under which the common run of men would become emaciated and gaunt, and which they would find demoralizing and intolerable. In similar circumstances, a sage would not despair or feel resentful, and would not lose sight of his source of inner joy. Why? Because inwardly he has that which links him with the trigger of heaven, and so does not give up what he finds in himself for the sake of position, wealth, and ease.[86]

Section 20

Hence, take the cawing of the crow [191]

    And the squawking of the magpie: [191]

Are these ever changed for the sake of the fluctuations of temperature and humidity? Hence, once what is got from *dao* is settled, I will not have to wait for the cycle of change with the myriad things. That by which I find it in myself is not determined by transient changes. What I mean by "finding it" is understanding the content of one's decreed nature, and dwelling in the peace they offer. The decreed nature issues forth from the ancestor at the same time as the physical form.

    When the physical form has the full complement of its parts,
        the decreed nature is complete. [192]
    And when the decreed nature is complete, likes and dislikes
        manifest themselves. [192]

Thus, the scholar is judged by agreed standards, and a woman follows unalterable conduct. Compasses and squares cannot improve upon the standards of the square and the circle, nor can the plumb line and the set square on the standards of angularity and straightness. The length of the cosmos is such that it does not become longer by measuring it from the top of a hill nor does it become shorter by measuring it from low ground. Hence, the person who has gained *dao*:

    Is not cowered in straitened circumstances,
    And does not bloom in the glow of success; [193]

處高而不機，
持盈而不傾，　　〔耕平〕　[193]
新而不朗，
久而不渝，　　　〔魚平〕　[194]
入火不焦，
入水不濡。　　　〔魚平〕　[194]
是故不待勢而尊，
不待財而富，
不待力而强，　　〔陽平〕　[195]
平虛下流，
與化翱翔。　　　〔陽平〕　[195]
若然者，藏金於山，
藏珠於淵，　　　〔眞平〕　[196]
不利貨財，
不貪勢名。　　　〔耕平〕　[196]
是故不以康爲樂，
不以慊爲悲，　　〔微平〕　[197]
不以貴爲安，
不以賤爲危，　　〔歌平〕　[197]
形神氣志，
各居其宜，　　　〔歌平〕　[197]
以隨天地之所爲。　〔歌平〕　[197]

夫形者，生之舍也；氣者，生之充也；神者，生之制也。一失〔其〕位，則二者傷矣。是故聖人使（人）各處其位，守其職，而不得相干也。

故夫形者非其所安也而處之則廢，　〔祭〕　　[198]
氣不當其所充〔也〕而用之則泄，　〔月〕　　[198]

130

He does not teeter when perched on high,
And keeps an even keel even when maintaining fullness; [193]
He is new without being shiny
And does not fade with the passage of time; [194]
He is not charred on entering fire
And is not soaked on entering water.[87] [194]

Hence, he is honored without reliance on position,
Affluent without relying on wealth,
Strong without relying on physical strength. [195]
Calm and empty, he flows downward,
And soars up and down with the demiurge of change. [195]
A person like this buries the gold in the mountains
And pearls in the depths. [196]
He is not tempted by goods and wealth,
And is not greedy after position and reputation.[88] [196]

Hence, he neither considers prosperity as joyous
Nor privation as sorrowful; [197]
He neither considers high position as secure
Nor lowliness as perilous. [197]
His physical form, his spirit and his energies,
Each is lodged in its proper place, [197]
Following the workings of the world. [197]

The physical form is the lodging house of life, *qi* is its stuff, and the spirit is its control. If one of these is deprived of its position, the other two are harmed. Hence, the sage makes each of these take its rightful place and keep to its own duties without interfering in those of the other two.

Thus, if one's physical form is placed in an unsuitable abode,
it will become incapacitated; [198]
If one's *qi* is made to fill what it does not rightfully fill, it will
be leaked; [198]

神非其所宜〔也〕而行之則昧。　　〔祭〕　　[198]

　　此三者，不可不慎守也。

　　夫舉天下萬物，蚑蟯貞蟲，蠕動蚑作，皆知其所喜憎利害
者，何也？以其性之在焉而不離也，忽去之，則骨肉無倫矣。
今人之所以眭然能視，瞥然能聽，形體能抗，而百節可屈伸，
察能分白黑、視醜美，而知能別同異、明是非者，何也？氣爲
之充，而神爲之使也。何以知其然也？凡人（之）志（各）有
所在而神有所繫者，其行也，足蹪趚垎、頭抵植木而不自知
也，招之而不能見也，呼之而不能聞也。耳目〔非〕去之也，
然而不能應者，何也？神失其守也。

故在於小則忘於大，　　〔祭〕　　[199]

在於中則忘於外，　　〔祭〕　　[199]

在於上則忘於下，

在於左則忘於右。　　〔之上〕　　[200]

無所不充，則無所不在。　　〔之上〕　　[200]

132

If one's spirit is active when it is not suited to act, it will grow
    dim. [198]

These three are what one should watch over carefully.

Section 21

All of the myriad things in the world down to the tiny bugs and
swarming insects squirming and wriggling about know what they like
and dislike, what will benefit them and cause them harm. Why? It is
because they have got their nature which has not deserted them.
Once their nature leaves them, they will be unable to know their own
kind. Now, man is able to see and hear with discernment, is able to
raise his body and lift his limbs, and can bend and stretch his joints;
in his discrimination he is able to distinguish white from black and
the beautiful from the ugly, and in his intelligence he can differentiate
sameness from difference and the right from the wrong. Why? Because his *qi* fills his body and his spirit is at his bidding. How do we
know this to be so? Because whenever the focus of a man's mind is
directed toward something and his spirit is bound up with something, then he can stumble over a stump or bang his head on a tree
without even being conscious of it. And if you try to beckon him, he
won't be able to see, and if you try to call him, he won't be able to
hear. It is not that his eyes and ears have deserted him, and yet he is
not able to respond. Why? It is because his spirit has left its station.

Thus, where the attention of the spirit is directed toward the
    small, it is oblivious to the big; [199]
Where it is directed toward the internal, it is oblivious to
    what's going on externally; [199]
Where it is directed toward what is above, it is oblivious to
    that below;
Where it is directed toward the left, it is oblivious to the
    right. [200]
It is only when there is no place that the spirit does not fill
    that there is nowhere toward which the focus is not
    directed. [200]

是故貴虛者以毫末爲宅也。

今夫狂者之不能避水火之難而越溝瀆之嶮者，豈無形神氣
志哉？然而用之異也。失其所守之位，而離其外內之舍，

是故舉錯不能當，	〔陽平〕	[201]	[A]
動靜不能中，	〔東平〕	[201]	[A]
終身運枯形于連嶁列埒之門，	〔諄平〕	[202]	[A]
而蹪蹈于污壑窄陷之中，	〔東平〕	[201]	[A]
雖生俱與人鈞，	〔眞平〕	[202]	[A]

然而不免爲人戮笑者，何也？形神相失也。

故以神爲主者，形從而利；	〔脂去〕	[203]
以形爲制者，神從而害。	〔祭〕	[203]
貪饕多欲之人，		
漠暗於勢利，	〔脂去〕	[203]
誘慕於（召）〔名〕位，	〔微去〕	[203]
冀以過人之智		
植（于高）〔高于〕世，	〔祭〕	[203]
則精神日以耗而彌遠，	〔元上〕	[204]

Hence, one who values emptiness takes the tip of an autumn
  hair as his abode.

Section 22

Now, the madman is unable to avoid the hazards of fire and
water and is unable to make his way over obstacles like ditches and
culverts. Surely it is not because he does not have a physical form, a
spirit, *qi*, and his purposes. It is that the way he uses them is different
so that they have lost the positions they should keep to and have allowed
themselves to be separated from their inner and outer abodes.

Hence, in every act he is inappropriate, [201]
And in every movement he is unable to hit the mark; [201]
All his life he drags his withered body along a dizzying
  precipice fraught with hazards, [202]
Ultimately to stumble headlong into some filthy ditch. [201]
Although as far as being alive is concerned he is the same as
  others, [202]

He cannot escape the scorn and ridicule of his fellows. Why? Because
his body and spirit have lost their position.

Thus, where the spirit is master, the body will go on to be
  benefited, [203]
But with the body in control, the spirit will go on to be
  harmed. [203]
Because a covetous and avaricious person
Is submerged in power and profit, [203]
And is engrossed in the desire for reputation and
  position, [203]
And hopes against hope that by means of surpassing
  cleverness
He can establish a high reputation in the world, [203]
His spirit is squandered day by day, and goes increasingly far
  afield. [204]

135

　　　　　　　　久淫而不還，　　〔元上〕　　[204]

形閉中距，則神無由入矣。是以天下時有盲妄自失之患。此膏
燭之類也，火逾然而消逾亟。夫精〔神〕氣志者，靜而（日）
充者〔日〕以壯，躁而（日）耗者〔日〕以老。是故聖人將養
其神，和弱其氣，平夷其形，而與道沉浮俛仰，

　　　　　　　　恬然則縱之，　　〔東去〕　　[205]

　　　　　　　　迫則用之。　　　〔東去〕　　[205]

　　　　　　其縱之也若委衣，　　〔微平〕　　[206]

　　　　　　其用之也若發機。　　〔微平〕　　[206]

如是則萬物之化無不遇，而百事之變無不應。

136

> If for a long time it wanders too far from home without
> coming back, [204]

The body will shut its apertures and resist from within, and there will be no way for the spirit to gain entry. Therefore, there are often cases of blindness, wildness, and the loss of sanity in the world. This is of a kind with the tallow torch in that the faster the fire burns, the quicker the tallow is exhausted. Now, where the spirit and the *qi* are tranquil and become daily fuller, the individual remains robust, but where they are agitated and daily squandered, the individual becomes aged. Hence, the sage nurtures his spirit, harmonizes and retains the fluency of his *qi*, calms his body, and sinks and floats, rises and falls with *dao*.

> Placidly, giving it its head, [205]
> When borne down upon, he makes use of it. [205]
> When he gives it its head, it is like shedding a coat; [206]
> In using it, it is like touching off a trigger. [206]

Thus, of the myriad transformations of things, there is none that he cannot match; of the hundred changes of affairs, there is none to which he cannot respond.

[1] Cf. *Zhuangzi* 19/6/89 and 34/13/13; cf. translation in Graham (1981):86 and Watson (1968):81 (hereafter G86 and W81 respectively).

[2] The eight points of the compass are N, NE, E, SE, S, SW, W, NW.

[3] Cf. *Daodejing* 4:

> *Dao* is empty, yet when used there is something that does not make it full.

Also *Daodejing* 15:

> The murky, being stilled, slowly becomes clear.

[4] The conjunctives 是故 , 故 , and 故以 more frequently than not mark an intentional break in the text rather than an inference. We have translated these as "hence," "thus," and "therefore" respectively, while at the same time introducing a break into the text.

[5] It was believed that the world is bounded by four seas.

[6] Cf. *Da Dai Liji* 4.4/30/4.

[7] Cf. *Daodejing* 36:

> If you would have a thing shrink,
> You must first stretch it out;
> If you would have a thing weakened,
> You must first strengthen it; . . .

[8] Cf. *Huainanzi* 15/144/17.

[9] Cf. *Daodejing* 39:

> Of old, these came to possess the One:
> Heaven possessed the One and became thereby limpid;
> Earth possessed the One and became thereby settled;
> Gods possessed the One and became thereby potent;
> The valley possessed the One and became thereby full;
> Lords and princes possessed the One and became thereby
> leaders of the empire.

[10] In some sources, these two emperors are identified as Fu Xi and Shen Nong, but in others, they are Fu Xi and Nü Wa.

[11] Cf. *Zhuangzi* 52/20/26 (G: not translated, W213).

[12] Cf. *Zhuangzi* 29/12/8 (G269, W127).

[13] Cf. *Liji* 19.22/102/13 and *Zhuangzi* 23/9/8 (G205, W105).

[14] Cf. *Liji* 19.22/102/14.

[15] "Evil confluences of the *yin* and the *yang*" is literally "rainbows."

[16] Cf. *Daodejing* 2, 10, and 51. In the *Daodejing* 10 parallel, *dao* itself becomes steward. See note 57.

[17] Cf. *Zhuangzi* 55/21/19–20 (G168, W223).

[18] Cf. *Daodejing* 14:

> Its upper part is not dazzling;
> Its lower part is not indistinct.
> Dimly visible, it cannot be named,
> And returns to that which is without substance.
> This is called the shape that has no shape,
> The image that is without substance.

And *Daodejing* 21:

> As a thing *dao* is
> Shadowy, indistinct.
> Indistinct and shadowy,
> Yet within it is an image;
> Shadowy and indistinct,
> Yet within it is a substance.
> Dim and dark,
> Yet within it is a quintessence.
> This quintessence is quite genuine.

[19] Ping Yi and Da Bing are legendary charioteers, who in most sources are identified as water gods. For example, the Lord of the River in *Zhuangzi* 17 is often identified as Ping Yi. The Gao You commentary identifies him as an historical person who drowned himself in the Yellow River to become a water immortal.

[20] Cf. *Daodejing* 27:

> One who is good at traveling leaves no wheel tracks.

[21] Cf. *Zhuangzi* 1/1/3 and 14 (G43 and 44, W29 and 31).

[22] The Kunlun Mountains, situated in the northwestern reaches of China, and Penglai off the coast of Shandong, were two principal Daoist paradises.

This mountain range held a central position in the mythology and popular religion of early China as the home of the Queen Mother of the West and a pantheon of gods, spirits, and humans who had achieved immortality. See Birrell (1993):183–185.

[23] The Changhe gates appear in early philosophical literature as a set of gates to the south of the palace of the High Ancestor, and are often identified as "the Gateway of Heaven."

[24] The Gateway of Heaven, like the Changhe gates, is the source from which the myriad things emerge. Hence, the opening and closing of these gates is a symbolic expression for the process of change itself. For example, the *Daodejing* 10 states:

> When the Gateway of Heaven opens and shuts
> Are you capable of keeping to the role of the female?

[25] Cf. *Daodejing* 38:

> Hence a great man abides in the thick not in the thin, in the fruit not in the flower.

[26] Cf. *Hanfeizi* 10.5.112.

[27] Cf. *Zhuangzi* 17/6/42 (G87, W83) and 21/7/32 (G98, W97).

[28] Cf. *Zhuangzi* 15/6/9 (G84–85, W77–78), 44/17/52 (G149, W182–183), 69/24/98 (G85, W277).

[29] Cf. *Zhuangzi* 29/12/17 (G272, W128).

[30] Cf. *Daodejing* 66:

> Therefore, the sage is in front of the multitude, yet they do not find he blocks the view; he is on top of the people, yet they do not find him heavy. The whole empire supports the sage joy-fully without ever tiring of doing so. It is because he does not contend that none are able to contend with him.

[31] Zhan He and Juan Xuan were famous fishermen. Zhan He was from the state of Chu. His interview with the king of Chu on angling appears in some detail in *Liezi*. He is so effective in using the small to control the large that, using a single thread of silk as his line, and without bending the rod, he is able to land a fish that fills an entire cart. See Graham (1960):105. See also *Huainanzi* 6/50/11, 12/109/21.

[32] A legendary bow that originally belonged to the Yellow Emperor, but was recovered by his subjects after it fell from his "dragon" chariot. See Sima Qian (1959):1394.

[33] Yi is the "Eastern Barbarian" who, as an archer of legendary prowess, was commanded by Emperor Yao to shoot the ten suns when they arose in the sky at the same time, scorching the earth. Feng Mengzi learned his skill at archery from Yi, but, blinded by his envy of Yi's superior ability, used a primitive club made out of peach wood (*tao* 桃) to batter Yi to death and thereby "expel (*tao* 逃)" his rival. See Birrell (1993):138–145.

[34] Cf. *Zhuangzi* 16/6/26 (G86, W80–81) and 64/23/74 (G: not translated, W260).

[35] Cf. *Daodejing* 14:

> Of the One . . .
>> This is called the shape that has no shape,
>> The image that is without substance.

And also *Daodejing* 41:

>> The great image has no shape.

[36] Gun of Xia was the father of Yu, the ruler who was able to control the floodwaters. One myth has Gun taking self-renewing earth from Heaven to dam up the flood without first getting permission, and then being killed for his crime, with Yu emerging from his belly. See Birrell (1993):146–159.

[37] See *Zuozhuan* Ai 7, Legge (1960):814 .

[38] Cf. *Zhuangzi* 31/12/56 (G186, W134).

[39] For the role of the battering ram in early Chinese military history, see Needham and Yates (1994):429–437.

[40] Yi Yin was first the cook and later the councillor to Tang, founder of the Shang, who defeated the House of Xia. See Birrell (1993):128–129, 195–196. Zao Fu is found throughout the early corpus as a charioteer of legendary prowess who served King Mu of the House of Zhou, and who took him on his famous trip to the west. His charioting in establishing a balance between driver and horses is a familiar metaphor for effective government.

[41] Cf. *Shenzi* 71:

> The clarity of Li Zhu's vision was such that he could distinguish the tip of a hair at more than one hundred paces, but

when he looked down into the water, even when it was only a foot deep, he could not fathom its depth. This is not because he could not see clearly, but because the circumstances made it difficult to see. [Based on P. Thompson's draft translation.]

[42] For a detailed discussion of the "eight winds" see the "Patterns of Heaven" treatise of the *Huainanzi* translated with commentary in Major (1993):77–79, and the notes in Kusuyama (1971):143.

[43] Music Master Kuang is symbolic of the virtuoso musician in the early corpus. See the translation of one among many anecdotes about him, and further references, in Le Blanc (1985):102.

[44] Shen Nong is a legendary ruler who is remembered as the sage who developed and taught husbandry. He is also the father of Chinese medicine, having devoted himself to the study of herbs and their properties. Shen Nong often stands in contrast to the Yellow Emperor because he is associated with tribal, agrarian government while the Yellow Emperor is an emblem of centralized, bureaucratic government.

[45] Cf. *Zhuangzi* 73/26/3 (G: not translated, W294–295).

[46] Cf. *Huainanzi* 3/22/14f.

[47] Cf. *Liji* 19.2/102/14.

[48] Cf. Liu Buwei (1955):672.

[49] Cf. *Liezi*, Graham (1960):99.

[50] Cf. *Zhuangzi* 33/13/5 (G259, W142–143); 40/15/8 (G265–266, W168–169).

[51] Cf. *Zhuangzi* 44/17/51 (G149, W183).

[52] Cf. *Zhuangzi* 42/17/5 (G145, W176).

[53] Cf. *Daodejing* 47:

> Therefore the sage knows without having to stir,
> Identifies without having to see,
> Accomplishes without having to act.

[54] Gong Gong, a mythical warrior who appears throughout the early corpus, brings disorder to the world through his quarrels. See Birrell (1993):97.

[55] See a similar story in *Zhuangzi* 77/28/15–18 (G226, W311).

[56] Cf. *Zhuangzi* 17/6/52 (G88, W84).

[57] Cf. *Daodejing* 10 for this expression *xuande*:

> It gives them life and rears them.
>
> It gives them life without claiming to possess them;
>
> It is the steward yet exercises no authority over them.
>
> Such is called dark virtue [*xuande*].

See also *Daodejing* 51 for a similar passage, and 65:

> Constantly to be aware of the models
>
> Is known as dark virtue [*xuande*].
>
> Dark virtue is profound and far-reaching,
>
> But when things turn back it turns back with them.
>
> Only then does it go completely with the stream.

[58] Cf. *Zhuangzi* 5/2/61 (G57, W45) and *Daodejing* 1.

[59] Cf. *Daodejing* 2, 37, 48.

[60] Cf. *Zhuangzi* 71/25/52 (G102, W288).

[61] Cf. *Daodejing* 3:

> Hence, in his rule, the sage empties their minds but fills their bellies, weakens their purpose but strengthens their bones.

[62] Cf. *Daodejing* 39:

> Hence, the exalted necessarily takes the lowly as root, and the lofty necessarily takes the base as foundation.

[63] Cf. *Daodejing* 76:

> A man is supple and weak when alive, but hard and stiff when dead. The myriad creatures and grass and trees are pliant and fragile when alive, but dried and shriveled when dead. Thus it is said, the hard and the strong are the comrades of death; the supple and the weak are the comrades of life.
>
> > Hence a weapon that is strong will not vanquish;
> >
> > A tree that is strong will come to its end;
> >
> > Thus the strong and big takes the lower position;
> >
> > The supple and weak takes the upper position.

[64] Cf. *Daodejing* 7:

> Hence the sage puts his person back and it comes to the fore,
>
> Treats his person as extraneous and it is preserved.

[65] Cf. *Zhuangzi* 71/25/51 (G102, W288) and 75/27/10 (G102, W305).

[66] Wang Niansun in his commentary suggests an alternative reading:

> This is a fact obvious to the most ordinary people and yet the
> superior and wise are not able to avoid falling into the trap.
> This is because they are blinkered.

[67] Cf. *Daodejing* 78:

> In the world there is nothing more submissive and weak than
> water. Yet for attacking that which is unyielding and strong
> nothing can take precedence over it. This is because there is
> nothing that can take its place.

[68] This quotation is almost identical to *Daodejing* 43.

[69] This expression is from *Daodejing* 50.

[70] See *Zhuangzi* 21/7/31 (G98, W97). Each clod of earth has its own unique
shape, and like the uncarved block, remains unadorned and resistant to
conventional valorizations.

For an explanation of this technical cosmological terminology, see Major
(1993), especially pp. 35–38.

[71] Cf. *Daodejing* 6:

> Tenuous, it seems as if it were there,
> Yet use will never exhaust it.

[72] Cf. *Daodejing* 14:

> Look at it and you do not see it—this you call minute;
> Listen to it and you do not hear it—this you call rarified;
> Feel for it and you do not get hold of it—this you call
> intangible.

and *Daodejing* 35:

> There is not enough of it, when looked at, to be visible,
> Nor is there enough of it, when listened to, to be audible.
> Yet use cannot exhaust it.

[73] Cf. *Daodejing* 15:

> Thick like the uncarved block;
> Murky like muddy water,
> Immense like a valley.
> The muddy, being stilled, slowly becomes limpid,
> The settled, being stirred, slowly comes to life.

[74] Cf. *Daodejing* 20.

[75] Cf. *Zhuangzi* 40/15/14 (G266, W169).

[76] Cf. *Zhuangzi* 25/11/4 (G211, W114).

[77] Cf. *Zhuangzi* 40/15/14–16 (G266, W169).

[78] Cf. *Zhuangzi* 15/6/5 (G84, W77).

[79] We follow Wang Niansun in omitting these four lines.

[80] Cf. *Hanfeizi* 21.21.1.

[81] Cf. *Daodejing* 20:

> The multitude are joyous
> As if partaking of the *tailao* offering
> While going on a terrace in spring.
> I alone am inactive and reveal no signs,
> Like a baby that has not yet learned to smile,
> Listless as though with no home to go back to.

[82] Cf. *Zhuangzi* 38/14/49 (G129, W161).

[83] Cf. *Xunzi* 2/1/30; cf. Knoblock (1988) vol 1:140.

[84] Cf. *Daodejing* 29:

> Now the empire is a sacred vessel. It is not a thing that can be
> put in order. He who puts it in order will ruin it; he who keeps
> his hold will lose it.

[85] This story occurs throughout *Zhuangzi*; see for example 2/1/22 (G45, W32) and 29/12/20 (G: not translated, W129–130).

[86] Cf. *Zhuangzi* 78/28/51 (G229, W317) and 65/24/17 (G: not translated, W263).

[87] Cf. *Zhuangzi* 2/1/33 (G46, W33), 15/6/5 (G84, W77), and 57/21/68 (G: not translated, W232).

[88] Cf. *Zhuangzi* 29/12/10 (G270–271, W127).

Allen, Sarah (1997). *The Way of Water and Sprouts of Virtue*. Albany: State University of New York Press.

Birrell, Anne (1993). *Chinese Mythology: An Introduction*. Baltimore: Johns Hopkins University Press.

Chou-i. (1935). Harvard-Yenching Institute Sinological Index Series, Supplement 10. Beijing: Harvard-Yenching.

Chuang Tzu. (1947). Harvard-Yenching Institute Sinological Index Series, Supplement 20. Beijing: Harvard-Yenching.

Elvin, Mark (1985). "Between the earth and heaven: conceptions of the self in China," in *The Category of the Person*. Edited by Michael Carrithers, Steven Collins, and Steven Lukes. Cambridge: Cambridge University Press.

Foucault, Michel (1973). *The Order of Things: An Archaeology of the Human Sciences*. New York: Vintage.

Gernet, Jacques (1983). *China and the Christian Impact: A Conflict of Cultures*. Cambridge: Cambridge University Press.

Graham, A. C. (trans) (1981). *Chuang-tzu: The Inner Chapters*. London: George Allen & Unwin.

Graham, A. C. (1960). *The Book of Lieh Tzu*. London: John Murray.

Hanfeizi suoyin. (1982). Edited by Zhou Zhongling et al. Beijing: Zhonghua shuju.

Hartman, Charles (1986). *Han Yü and the T'ang Search for Unity*. Princeton: Princeton University Press.

Hay, John (1994). "The Persistent Dragon (*lung*)," in *The Power of Culture: Studies in Chinese Cultural History*. Edited by W. Peterson, A. Plaks, Y.S. Yu. Princeton: Princeton University Press.

——— (1993). "The Human Body as a Microcosmic Source of Macrocosmic Values in Calligraphy," in *Self as Body in Asian Theory and Practice*. Edited by T.P. Kasulis, R.T. Ames, and W. Dissanayake. Albany: State University of New York Press.

Ho, Che Wah 何志華. "Chutu *Wenzi* xinzheng" (New evidence from the *Wenzi* excavated at Ding County), in *Sino-Humanitas* No. 5 (1998).

Hsün Tzu. (1950). Harvard-Yenching Institute Sinological Index Series, Supplement 22. Beijing: Harvard-Yenching.

Jullien, François (1995). *The Propensity of Things: Toward a History of Efficacy in China.* New York: Zone Books.

Knoblock, John (trans) (1994). *Xunzi: A Translation and Study of the Complete Works.* Vol 3. Stanford: Stanford University Press.

———— (1988). *Xunzi: A Translation and Study of the Complete Works.* Vol 1. Stanford: Stanford University Press.

Kusuyama, Haruki (trans) (1971). *Enanji* Vol 1. Tokyo: Meitoku Shuppansha.

Lau, D. C. (trans) (1983). *Confucius: The Analects.* Hong Kong: Chinese University Press.

———— (trans) (1982). *Tao Te Ching.* Hong Kong: Chinese University Press.

Lau, D. C., and Roger T. Ames (1996). *Sun Pin: The Art of Warfare.* New York: Ballantine.

Lau, D. C., and Chen Fong Ching (editors) (1992). *A Concordance to the Dadai Liji.* ICS Ancient Chinese Text Concordance Series. Hong Kong: Commercial Press.

———— (1992). *A Concordance to the Huainanzi.* ICS Ancient Chinese Text Concordance Series. Hong Kong: Commercial Press.

———— (1992). *A Concordance to the Liji.* ICS Ancient Chinese Text Concordance Series. Hong Kong: Commercial Press.

Le Blanc, Charles (1985). *Huai-nan Tzu: Philosophical Synthesis in Early Han Thought.* Hong Kong: Hong Kong University Press.

Legge, James (1960). *The Chinese Classics in Five Volumes.* Vol V, *The Ch'un Ts'ew with The Tso Chuen.* Hong Kong: Hong Kong University Press.

Li Zehou (1987). *Li Zehou zhexue meixue wenxuan.* Taibei: Gufeng Publishers. Translated by Gong Lizeng (1994) as *The Path of Beauty: A Study of Chinese Aesthetics.* Hong Kong: Oxford University Press.

Liu Buwei (1955). *Lüshi chunqiu.* Edited by Xu Weiyu. Taibei: Shijie shuju.

Liu Wendian (1933). *Huainan Honglie jijie.* Shanghai: Commercial Press.

Loewe, Michael (1986). "The Former Han Dynasty" in *The Cambridge History of China*. Vol I, *The Ch'in and Han Empires 221 BC–AD 220*. Cambridge: Cambridge University Press.

Major, John S. (1993). *Heaven and Earth in Early Han Thought: Chapters Three, Four, and Five of the Huainanzi*. Albany: State University of New York Press.

Mencius (*Meng Tzu*). (1941). Harvard-Yenching Institute Sinological Index Series, Supplement 17. Beijing: Harvard-Yenching.

Needham, Joseph, and Robin D.S. Yates, et al. (1994). *Science and Civilisation in China*. Vol V, Part VI. Cambridge: Cambridge University Press.

Roth, Harold D. (1992). *The Textual History of the Huai-nan Tzu*. Ann Arbor: The Association for Asian Studies.

Rorty, Richard (1979). *Philosophy and the Mirror of Nature*. Princeton: Princeton University Press.

Ryle, Gilbert (1949). *The Concept of Mind*. London: Hutchinson.

Sima Qian (1959). *Records of the Historian* (*Shiji*). Shanghai: Zhonghua shuju.

Thompson, Paul M. (1979). *The Shen Tzu Fragments*. Oxford: Oxford University Press.

Tu Wei-ming (1997). "Chinese Philosophy: A Synopsis," in *A Companion to World Philosophies*. Edited by Eliot Deutsch and Ron Bontekoe. Oxford: Blackwell.

Wang Niansun. See Liu Wendian.

Watson, Burton (trans) (1968). *The Complete Works of Chuang Tzu*. New York: Columbia University Press.

Xunzi. See *Hsün Tzu* and Knoblock.

Yates, Robin D.S. (1997). *Five Lost Classics: Tao, Huang-Lao, and Yin-yang in Han China*. New York: Ballantine.

Yijing. See *Chou-i*.

Zhang, Dongsun (1995). *Zhishi yu wenhua: Zhang Dongsun wenhua lunzhu jiyao*. Edited by Zhang Yaonan. Beijing: Zhongguo guangbo dianshi chubanshe.

Zhuangzi. See *Chuang Tzu*.